Theos – clear thinking on religion

Theos is the UK's leading religion and society think tank. With our ideas
a combined circulation of 160 million in the past 5 years, we are shapin
about the role of faith in contemporary society by means of high qualit
We provide a credible, informed and gracious Christian voice in our mainstream public conversations.

The Economist calls us "an organisation that demands attention", and Julian Baggini, the influential atheist philosopher, has said "Theos provides rare proof that theology can be interesting and relevant even – perhaps especially – for those who do not believe."

To learn more, check us out on social media:

twitter.com/theosthinktank | facebook.com/theosthinktank | www.theosthinktank.co.uk

Why we exist

Religion has emerged as one of the key public issues of the 21st century, both nationally and globally. Our increasingly religiously-diverse society demands that we grapple with religion as a significant force in public life. Unfortunately, much of the debate about the role and place of religion has been unnecessarily emotive and ill-informed. We exist to change that.

We reject the notion of any possible 'neutral' perspective on these issues. We also reject the idea that religion is a purely private matter or that it is possible to divide public and private values for anyone.

We seek, rather, to recognise and analyse the ethical ideas and commitments that underlie public life and to engage in open and honest public debate, bringing the tradition of Christian social and political thought to bear on current issues. We believe that the mainstream Christian tradition has much to offer for a flourishing society.

What we do

Theos conducts research, publishes reports, and holds debates, seminars and lectures on the intersection of religion, politics and society in the contemporary world. We also provide regular comment for print and broadcast media and briefing and analysis to parliamentarians and policy makers. To date, Theos has produced over 50 research reports focusing on the big issues impacting British society, including welfare (*The Future of Welfare: A Theos Collection*), law (*"Speaking Up" – Defending and Delivering Access to Justice Today*), economics (*Just Money: How Catholic Social Teaching can Redeem Capitalism*), multiculturalism (*Making Multiculturalism Work) and voting* reform (*Counting on Reform*), as well as on a range of other religious, legal, political and social issues.

In addition to our independently-driven work, Theos provides research, analysis and advice to individuals and organisations across the private, public and not-for-profit sectors. Our staff and consultants have strong public affairs experience, an excellent research track record and a high level of theological literacy. We are practised in research, analysis, debate, and media relations.

Where we sit

We are committed to the traditional creeds of the Christian faith and draw on social and political thought from a wide range of theological traditions. We also work with many non-Christian and non-religious individuals and organisations.

Theos was launched with the support of the Archbishop of Canterbury and the Cardinal Archbishop of Westminster, but it is independent of any particular denomination. We are an ecumenical Christian organisation, committed to the belief that religion in general and Christianity in particular has much to offer for the common good of society as a whole. We are not aligned with any point on the party political spectrum, believing that Christian social and political thought cuts across these distinctions.

Join the discussion by becoming a Friend of Theos

Impact how society views Christianity and shape the cultural debate

The Friends' Programme is designed specifically for people who wish to enter the heart of the current debate. When you join, our commitment is to keep you informed, equipped, encouraged and inspired so that you can be a voice in the public square with us.

As a member of the Friends' Programme, you are provided with:

- *Hard copies of all our latest reports* on the most pressing issues – social justice, welfare, politics, spirituality, education, money, atheism, humanism…
- *Free access to our events.* Theos hosts a number of high calibre speakers (e.g. Rowan Williams, Larry Siedentop, Grace Davie) and debates ('Magna Carta and the future of liberty', 'Does humanism need Christianity?'). As a friend, you will receive invitations to all these without charge.
- *A network of like-minded people* who wish to share ideas and collaborate with one another. We host networking events which help you meet fellow Friends and build your own network, allowing ideas to flow and connections to form.
- *Our monthly e-newsletter* which is your one-stop digest for the latest news regarding religion and society.
- If you join as an Associate, you are *invited to private functions with the team*, allowing you to discuss upcoming projects, review the latest issues and trends in society, and have your say in where you see the public debate is going.

You can become a Friend or Associate today by visiting our website
www.theosthinktank.co.uk

If you'd prefer additional information, you can write to us directly:
Friends Programme, Theos, 77 Great Peter Street, London, SW1P 2EZ

If you have any inquiries regarding the Programme, you can email us at:
friends@theosthinktank.co.uk

Passing on Faith

Olwyn Mark

Published by Theos in 2016
© Theos

ISBN 978-0-9931969-6-6

Some rights reserved – see copyright licence for details
For further information and subscription details please contact:

Theos
Licence Department
77 Great Peter Street
London
SW1P 2EZ

T 020 7828 7777
E hello@theosthinktank.co.uk
www.theosthinktank.co.uk

contents

acknowledgements   6

foreword   7

executive summary   11

introduction   14

chapter 1   religion and youth: a failure in transmission?   24

chapter 2   faith in the family: how it is passed on   35

chapter 3   passing on family faith: what makes a difference?   43

conclusion   61

bibliography   65

acknowledgements

I would like to thank Nick Spencer, Professor Trevor Cooling and Dr Bill Lattimer for their encouragement, partnership and support in the writing of this report. Their steering and contributions have significantly strengthened the final piece of work.

I would also like to thank Revd Dr Howard Worsley, Professor Robert Beckford, Dr Beth Green and Professor Christian Smith for their generous insights along the way.

My final thanks must go to my own parents, who passed on their Christian faith with unstinting devotion and sincerity. Faith, outworked in word and deed, was an integral part of our family life, and was nurtured in a home interwoven with love and stability. In light of this enduring influence, this report is dedicated to my father, Douglas Mark, who died on 19 September 2016. In life, he affirmed – with deep conviction – the attributes and promises of God. In the face of illness and death, he remained fully confident in the living hope that comes through the good news of Jesus Christ. It is with deep joy and gratitude that I, too, choose to live in the light of that same hope.

foreword

passing on faith today – what we know

What do parents think about passing on their faith – or, more broadly, the beliefs (or lack of them) about God – to the children? As part of this project, we commissioned the polling company ComRes to assess the view of parents (specifically parents of children under 18) concerning the spiritual nurture of children. Did they see it as a privilege, a priority, or just a problem?[1]

The answer was reasonably clear. When asked whether they would want their children "to hold the same beliefs about whether or not there is a God or Higher Power as me when they are older", less than a third (31%) of British parents agreed, and nearly twice as many (59%) disagreed. Passing on faith was not a priority, and this translated into parents' answers when asked whether it was *important* "to actively pass on beliefs about whether or not there is a God or Higher Power to [their] children" – the same proportion (30%) saying it was important, compared with twice that number (60%) saying that children should make up their own minds on this topic "independently of their parents".

If these were the headline figures, it is important to show that not all parents felt quite the same way about this – although it is also important to emphasise that one must be cautious here as the sample size of these sub-groups of respondents is much smaller and may therefore only be read as indicative. Those parents who were agnostic[2] or indifferent[3] about God were considerably less bothered about the children holding their beliefs (9% and 15% respectively). Atheists[4] were not significantly more bothered either (19%). By comparison, 59% of those who did "believe in a God"[5] wanted their children to share their beliefs. The same balance was seen when the data were analysed by attendance: regular attenders[6] were most likely to want to pass their beliefs on (77%), non-attenders[7] hardly at all (15%).

The picture was subtly different by self-defined religious group. Whereas, as expected from the above data, "Nones"[8] were not especially bothered whether their children adopted their beliefs (only 15%), self-defined Christians were only slightly above the national average, with 36% wanting to pass on their beliefs (compared to an average of

31%). A somewhat higher proportion of 'Other Religions' (69%)[9] wanted their children to hold their beliefs, and a higher still proportion of self-defined Muslims (85%) – although it is important to realise that this last figure was from a sub-sample size of only 57, which is too small to be reliable.[10]

The problem with these data, however, is the widely-recognised capaciousness of self-definition, particularly when it comes to the term 'Christian'. When the data were broken down further for 'Christians'[11], 57% of those self-defined Christians who believed in God[12] said that they would like their children to hold the same beliefs (about God or Higher Power) when they are older, and 69% of those Christians who attended church once a month or more[13] felt the same way. In other words, the more engaged Christians were with their faith, the more likely they were to want to pass it on to their children (though this is not to overlook the fact that nearly a third (28%) of church-attending Christians did not mind whether their children share their beliefs).

The issue, at least according to respondents themselves, was not so much that they felt uncomfortable passing on their faith to their children: two thirds (67%) of all parents said that they would feel "confident" in having a conversation on the subject with their children, and the same proportion (69%) said they would feel "comfortable" in doing so. It was simply that the subject rarely came up, with only 40% of parents saying they had had a conversation with the aim of passing on their beliefs about whether there is a God or Higher Power with their children – although again the more seriously the parents took their faith, the more likely they were to have spoken about it.

That noted, there were some specific problems that a sizeable minority of parents continually raised. Of least concern (for only 15% of parents) was the fear that they "wouldn't know how to start the conversation", with about the same number of parents (16%) feeling that they "may be doing something ethically wrong" and might be putting them off (17%). Nearly one in five parents (18%) positively said that it was "not my role as a parent to pass on my beliefs to my children",[14] whereas about one in four (23%) said that they were worried that they might be alienated at school, and the same proportion said they were concerned that their children "may have questions I couldn't answer" (26%). By some way, the greatest concern parents had was about social media, over a third (34%) saying that they felt that "technology and social media would have more of an impact on my children's beliefs than my input."

A sense of powerless is undoubtedly a mark of parenthood throughout the ages, but one wonders whether it is particularly intense today. Whether or not that is the case, it is certainly true that with a commitment to passing on faith comes anxiety, as pretty much every one of the concerns mentioned above was felt more by religious parents, in particular by church-attending Christians, but rather less by atheists, agnostics and the generally indifferent. This will naturally be a part of holding something to be important and therefore being concerned about the manner in which it is passed to children, but it may also reflect a normalising element within culture, whereby the seriously religious feel that passing on their beliefs in a generally more agnostic or secular culture is somehow harder or even less proper.

The fact that British culture is more agnostic, indifferent or even actively secular today than it was a generation or two ago is hard to deny, and it is probably that fact above any other that is shaping parental views on passing on faith. However, the fact the general culture may be more ambivalent about religious and spiritual issues does not necessarily mean children themselves are. Indeed, the evidence of recent years has increasingly come to the recognition that children are, in fact, innately spiritual – maybe even natural born believers.

Whichever way we interpret these data, the evidence gathered and analysed in this report is clear: however seriously parents take their responsibilities to pass on their beliefs, what they believe, say and do does have an incalculable impact on what their children end up believing. As Olwyn Mark puts it, the passing on of 'faith' invariably happens in every home. The challenge before any parent who cares about what their children ends up believing is to pass on those beliefs with guidance, love and integrity.

Nick Spencer
Research Director, Theos

references – foreword

1   ComRes interviewed 1,013 GB parents with children aged 18 and under online between 24 and 29 August 2016. Overall data were weighted to be representative of all GB adults aged 18+. ComRes is a member of the British Polling Council and abides by its rules (www.britishpollingcouncil.org).

2   "I am not sure about whether a God exists"; unweighted sample size: 212.

3   "I don't see this subject as relevant to my life at the moment"; unweighted sample size: 107.

4   "I don't believe in a God"; unweighted sample size: 271.

5   Unweighted sample size: 376.

6   i.e. "Once a week or more often" or "2-3 times a month"; weighted sample size: 142.

7   Weighted sample size: 519.

8   i.e. people who say they do not belong to any religion.

9   Unweighted sample: 113.

10   NB. unweighted sample sizes here are respectively 423 (Nones), 458 (Christian) and 57 (Muslim).

11   Sub-sample sizes meant this wasn't possible for other religious groups.

12   Yes: only 55% of Christians said they believed in God, 24% being unsure and 9% not believing.

13   Unweighted sample size: 102.

14   There is a curious anomaly in the data here; religious parents were more likely to agree with this than non-religious ones, despite the fact that they were keener to do just that. However, this may simply reflect the fact that religious parents were generally more concerned about passing on their faith, as noted in the following paragraph.

executive summary

- British parents are generally not too bothered about whether their children go on to share their beliefs, only 31% saying that they want their children "to hold the same beliefs about whether or not there is a God or Higher Power as me when they are older".

- Those parents who were agnostic or indifferent about God were least bothered (9% and 15% respectively), and atheists only slightly more (19%).

- Self-defined Christian parents were only slightly keener than average (36% vs. 31%) that their children shared their beliefs.

- A somewhat higher proportion of 'Other Religions' (69%) wanted their children to hold their beliefs, and a higher still proportion of self-defined Muslims (85%) – although it is important to realise that this last figure was from a sub-sample size of only 57, which is too small to be reliable.

- By contrast, 69% of those Christians who attended church once a month or more said they wanted their children to go on to share their belief.

- Overall, less than half (40%) of parents said they had had a conversation on the topic with their children although two thirds (67%) of all parents said that they would feel "confident" in having that conversation.

- By far the greatest concern to parents on this issues was social media, with over a third (34%) saying that they felt that "technology and social media would have more of an impact on my children's beliefs than my input."

- The passing on of 'faith' invariably happens in every home. This involves the transmission – both actively and passively – of values, attitudes, beliefs and practices. These can be associated with a particular religious tradition or independent of any one institutional system of belief. No child enters adolescence and adulthood unaffected by the overarching story that they learn in the home.

- When it comes to the passing on of faith in the home, this report does not uncover any new secret formulas or foolproof practices that will improve the likelihood of successful faith transmission. Instead, by means of an extensive study of the existing literature on this subject, *Passing on Faith* reinforces that which has been advanced for years by those involved in children's ministry within the Christian tradition. The assimilation of research studies in this report confirms that:

  - foundations for faith are laid in childhood;

  - the role and responsibility of the family is central in faith transmission (a theological assertion as well as an observation of child development theory);

  - enduring adolescent and adult believers are largely the product of caring, supportive, stable homes, where faith is seen, heard and experienced;

  - modelling is key: parents need to 'be' and 'do' what they want their child to become.

- This report assimilates and presents the findings of 54 published studies, each investigating what makes a difference in the home when it comes to passing on faith. The small and large-scale studies, published over the past 40 years, draw on multiple survey data collected among thousands of young people, parents and grandparents in the US, Canada, the UK, Sweden and Australia. While the majority of studies focus on mainstream Christian denominations, findings are also drawn from within Seventh-day Adventist, Jewish, Muslim, Sikh and Hindu communities.

- Research reveals that high quality relationships in the home are key to successful faith transmission: Adolescents and young adults who experience or who have experienced close, affirming, and accepting relationships with both parents are more likely to identify with the beliefs and practices of their parents. The security and stability of the parent-child relationship, including the strength of the childhood attachment, informs the stability of future religious beliefs.

- The style of parenting also makes a difference: Authoritative parenting – where the exercise of discipline and control is accompanied by warmth, nurture and responsiveness – is more conducive to religious transmission than authoritarian or permissive parenting.

- What is noteworthy from recent findings is that the nurturing role and faith commitment of both parents matters in faith transmission, i.e. it's not just the mother's job. Also, the role and influence of grandparents should not be underestimated.

- This report also comes with a gentle 'spiritual health' warning for parents: the integrity of your relationships and the consistency of your beliefs and practices matter. Both are found to positively correlate with the religious practices of adolescent and adult offspring.

- Parental unity, as evidenced in marital stability and the sharing of beliefs and practices, impacts on faith transmission.

- In view of changes in young people's religious involvement, more detailed research is needed to explore the priority of religious transmission in the home and the content of what is being passed on. This is in light of evidence that would suggest there is a lack of priority given, at least among some Christian parents, to passing on faith in the home.

- A response to generational decline in religious commitment calls for clear and confident articulation of teaching and traditions within faith communities.

- Overall, despite the perceived strength of other social and cultural forces, 'faith's' most effective 'not-so-secret' weapon in passing on beliefs and practices to the next generation remains parents.

introduction

There are many things that a good parent is expected to teach their child – from healthy eating to regular teeth brushing, mastering the times tables to respecting difference, and not forgetting, of course, good manners. There are no shortage of books and websites, with top-tips and keys to success. Indeed, cultural 'experts' weigh heavily on the consciences of parents at any and every stage of their child's development.

Ultimately, what we prioritise to teach our children is informed by what we consider to be important for their overall nurture and well-being.

To illustrate, a voice of popular parenting culture, *Mumsnet*, hailed as the UK's most popular parenting network, recently published in their education section '6 ways to teach your kids about road safety'.[1] These included tips on how to make the message stick through play, music and the repetition of rules and practices. Most important was example-setting and practising what you preach. As one parent noted, "I stood waiting ages today at a clear crossing for the green man. If we had gone, it would have taught my daughter that you don't always have to wait for the green man." In light of their advice, patience, creativity and consistency appear to be just a few of the qualities needed to teach a child to safely cross a busy road.

Of course, keeping a child safe is a priority of any competent parent, and any advice on how to do that more effectively is no doubt gratefully received. But is the same amount of attention given to the spiritual care and nurture of a child? Successful parents, it would seem, raise confident, healthy, open-minded and independent children. But do they raise spiritually-aware children? If they do, a parenting forum might ask the following: What are six ways to explore spiritual purpose with a child, or to nurture trust and loyalty in an overarching spiritual story? What are the top-tips for assisting a child to know and relate to God?

It is unclear whether nurturing the spiritual nature of a child is popularly classified as good parenting. For while packing a healthy snack for break time or teaching a child to safely cross the road undoubtedly are, practices which promote spiritual curiosity, wonder and faithfulness are a little more contentious.

the spiritual child: 'born believers'?

Exploring the spiritual nature of a child includes understanding the development of moral and religious thinking. Consequently, there is a burgeoning interest in the study of religion, spirituality and childhood within psychology. This is noted by the inclusion for the first time in the *Handbook of Child Psychology*, a chapter on religious and spiritual development.[2] The flourishing of this topic is evidently welcomed within the discipline:

> First, by studying children, psychologists of religion not only will achieve a better understanding of children but also a more comprehensive grasp of the origins of religiosity and spirituality as well as religion's role across the life span. Second, this sudden attention to children's religion and spirituality will help developmental psychologists arrive at a richer understanding of this fundamental, but neglected, dimension of development.[3]

Psychologists point to an inherent propensity of the child towards the spiritual. This includes a 'relational consciousness' that is not confined to a particular religious doctrine, but accords with a relational nature that connects to something larger than the self.[4] Included in this is a child's concept of God. Professor Justin Barrett, Director of the Thrive Center for Human Development at Fuller Seminary in the US, adopts this 'preparedness' hypothesis in his observations of the religious cognition of children. He argues that we are all in fact 'born believers'.[5] This suggests that we have a specific framework of thinking within which we understand the concept of the divine or spiritual.

Psychologists point to an inherent propensity of the child towards the spiritual.

This contradicts other accounts of the origin of religion, which state that a child's concept of God and the spiritual is a result of indoctrination rather than a matter of intuition. Instead of a natural propensity for belief in the supernatural, adults exploit the fact that "for good evolutionary reasons, children are highly credulous, and believe anything that the adults in their immediate circle tell them".[6] While agreeing with the tendency of children to trust their parents and other adults, Barrett responds to this position by noting that children are not likely to believe everything their parents teach them. Nor are all ideas equally well-received:

> Good luck teaching a five-year-old that people don't really have conscious minds or that it is okay to murder the neighbours in their sleep. The preponderance of scientific evidence (peer-reviewed and published) shows that some ideas find in children's minds infertile ground, whereas others readily grow and flourish.[7]

Faith, by Barrett's reckoning, is far more natural than some critics imagine, children intuitively inhabiting a spiritual frame rather than being dragged their by religious parents.

faith development in childhood

The discipline of psychology offers further insights into the development of faith in the child. Theories around religious and spiritual development in childhood have been shaped, in particular, by 'cognitive development' theories from mainstream psychology, for example, the four developmental stages of Piaget's theory on cognitive reasoning.[8] Piaget's theory presents four distinct and universal stages of cognitive maturation, stages in which a child or young person learns to assimilate and accommodate new information. At each stage, mental processes are re-ordered according to the new knowledge. Basic mental structures at birth develop into the advanced cognitive abilities of adolescence and emerging adulthood, where hypotheses and abstract concepts can be considered.

James Fowler's *Stages of Faith* outlines one such example of the adaption of this stage theory.[9] In the first intuitive stage of a child's faith development, ideas about God are normally picked up from family and the surrounding environment. Consequently, the importance of the home, and the role that it plays from the earliest stage of a child's faith development, is emphasised: "It is here that faith is first sensed, is born, and is nurtured."[10] The process of identity formation and development continues into adolescence, when the parental relationship remains of primary importance.[11] In view of this theory, Christian commentators have drawn not only on Scripture and Church tradition, but on developmental science, in giving an account of the nurture and development of faith. This natural capacity for faith, as such, is seen as part of God's gift in creation.[12]

Nevertheless, it is important to note that understanding faith development through the lens of psychology has its limitations. For one, it may offer only a reductionist, cognitive-centred understanding of human nature and religious experience, perhaps at the expense of the affective or emotional. In addition, an approach to understanding religious growth in 'stages' does not fully reflect the 'complexity and uniqueness' of faith development in the life of the individual.[13] Nor, indeed, does it fully reflect the impact of the social environment on this process. Importantly, adopting a scientific framework in which to observe faith development only asks the 'how' questions. It cannot give an account of the 'why'.

> Parents have a significant role to play at each and every stage of their child's faith development.

Yet despite these limitations, we will proceed on the following premises: that the child has an innate, observable spiritual nature; the development of this nature, and the thinking that accompanies it, can be understood in stages; and as we will come on to discuss, the nurturing of a child's spiritual nature is arguably essential for their overall well-being. Parents have a significant role to play at each and every stage of their child's faith development.

no neutrality in the home

We have hinted already in our discussion that the idea of 'passing on faith' is an unpalatable one for some. The notion that a child is 'religious', or even identified with a particular religion from birth, grates against a perceived 'neutral' and rationalistic account of the world. It is assumed that such labelling is incompatible with raising children to be open-minded and think for themselves. This would suggest that while teaching your child to cross the road safely is uncontentious, teaching your child about God is more so.

A secularist like Richard Dawkins draws a distinction between the participation in mere "harmless traditions" and the anti-rationalist proposition of "forcing" on children "un-evidenced opinions about the nature of life or the cosmos."[14] Indeed, if this "indoctrination of children before they reach the age of reason" were abandoned, suggests AC Grayling, the world may well move on from religious belief altogether.[15] It curiously follows that the teaching in the home of culturally approved, un-evidenced, 'neutral' values such as tolerance and respect is still welcomed; yet the expressed aspiration to 'pass on' religious beliefs and values is viewed as morally problematic.

Nonetheless, any parent who engages in any serious reflection on what they teach their child and why they teach him or her must at least answer the following: What information and skills do I want my child to learn, what attitudes and values do I want them to adopt, what virtues do I want them to cultivate, and why are these important? The *why* answer is shaped by a parent's own value system – their understanding of the world around them, and the meaning and purpose they attach to their own life and to that of their child. Parents navigate the competing voices, and fluctuating cultural messages, through the filter of their own beliefs and values, which in turn shape their attitudes and practices.[16]

The values that emerge are evidenced, for example, in their political persuasions, their approach to work, to leisure activities, to charitable activity, to neighbours, to money, to food, to drink – indeed, to pretty much everything they do, in the home and beyond. Such beliefs and values also shape an understanding of authority, responsibility, fairness and equality, care and compassion.

Importantly, the beliefs and values in the home may be associated with a religious tradition or judged independent of any one institutional system of belief. However, they do not emerge out of a vacuum, for there is no 'neutral' space in the home. Central to the discussion in this report is the understanding that parents invariably pass their values and beliefs on to their children – both intentionally *and* unintentionally – as the home remains the most effective channel of socialisation. As such, in directing our attention in this report to studies that largely concern families that are associated with a religious tradition, it is important not to lose sight of the fact that every family has a belief system or 'faith' that informs their internal and external purpose and practices.

nurturing the spiritual

Evidence would suggest that failing to nurture the spiritual identity of a child, may be the more damaging course of action.

Despite the apparent objections to 'passing on faith', evidence would suggest that failing to nurture the spiritual identity of a child, whether within a religious tradition or outside of it, may in fact be the more damaging course of action.

As the Theos meta-study *Religion and Well-being: Assessing the evidence* shows, by drawing on over 140 academic studies from the last thirty years, there is powerful evidence to suggest that the relationship between religion and spirituality and well-being is strong and positive, both for adolescents and for adults.[17] A close relationship with God and involvement in a religious community, for example, has been correlated with both positive mental health and lower substance use.[18] Furthermore, religion 'fosters the development and exercise of self-control and self-regulation',[19] is evidenced to reduce risk-taking behaviours among adolescents,[20] and acts as a buffer against the anxieties of life and the fear of death.[21] It has also been shown to maintain and enhance interpersonal relationships in the family.[22]

This, of course, is not to promote an instrumentalist approach towards religion – i.e. we pass on religious beliefs and practices in order to produce happy and healthy children. Nor, indeed, can we or should we adopt a compartmentalised view of the child – i.e. that their spiritual nature and nurture can somehow be separated from their overall personhood and welfare. These correlations of well-being and religion are just that – correlations, and not direct or definite associations. Nor, significantly, do these correlations address ultimate life questions, or decipher the truth claims of any one religious tradition.

Quenching spiritual curiosity and enquiry inhibits a child's opportunity to question fundamental truths claims about their world.

What these findings do provide, however, is a clear challenge to the assumption that nurturing the spiritual identity of a child, and seeking to 'pass on faith', is somehow dangerous or damaging for the child. We can assume that 'religion' broadly conceived fosters well-being, and denying encounters with it risks closing down an important avenue of their developı importantly, quenching spiritual curiosity and enquiry inhibits a child's oppo. ̤ ιο question fundamental truths claims about their world. Moreover, it dismisses ɩne life-transforming opportunity to encounter 'life in all its fullness'.

passing on faith: the challenge for the Church

Our discussion of the spiritual nature, nurture and development of a child – with a view to passing on and adopting faith – is set against the backdrop of an evident decline in Christian affiliation and church attendance in the UK.

The *Report of the Commission on Religion and Belief in Public Life* reported a threefold change in religion and belief in Britain in recent decades:

> The first is the increase in the number of people with non-religious beliefs and identities. The second is the decline in Christian affiliation, belief and practice and within this decline a shift in Christian affiliation that has meant that Anglicans no longer comprise a majority of Christians. The third is the increase in the number of people who have a religious affiliation but who are not Christian.[23]

Of particular note for this report is the finding from the Church of England's Church Growth Research Programme that half of the children of churchgoing parents do not attend as adults.[24] A generational change in religiosity is perceived to be the key reason for religious decline in modern Britain.[25] This presents a clear challenge for the future of the British church if the following assumption is adopted: "Retaining children/ youth is critical; it is easier to raise people as churchgoers than to turn the unchurched into attenders."[26] This position is further enforced by the expectation that religious beliefs and practices are largely settled by the time an individual reaches their early 20s and "if they are not religiously inclined in their youth they are unlikely to become so in later years."[27] Indeed, a recent study suggests that only two percent of Anglicans in England and Wales are converts.[28]

There are a multitude of theses on the cause and consequence of numerical decline in British church affiliation and attendance,[29] which in itself is not a recent phenomenon.[30] Indeed, it is argued that lack of affiliation is not equated with lack of belief, a position which is exemplified in Grace Davie's 'believing without belonging' thesis.[31] Nevertheless, when it comes to the decline in religious commitment, questions invariably arise over what factors contribute to successful or unsuccessful transmission. These are not just lines of inquiry for the social scientist, or questions of interest for the moral and social philosopher, but are of understandable concern for the devout parent.

conclusion

In view of this apparent trend, it is the family, and more specifically parents, as crucial channels of religious socialisation, around which this report revolves. The family is credited to be the context where faith is defined and experienced.[32]

The family is credited to be the context where faith is defined and experienced.

From a sociological perspective, not enough is known about the process of religious transmission in the home.[33] This could be on account of the fact that the ethnographic observations needed for such research raise particular practical and ethical challenges.[34] Nevertheless, while the process is difficult to evaluate, research has been done to assess the outcomes of religious transmission in the family.

Therefore, alongside a discussion on the changing shape of the relationship between young people and religion, and the continued importance of the home in religious socialisation, this report will assimilate, analyse and present the findings of research into the most successful ways for parents and the family to 'pass on' their faith to their children, in the process helping them to develop and secure their own.

The research will include studies from within the UK, and international studies, particularly from within a Western context, which might offer insights relevant to the UK. This encompasses data focussed not only on the Christian faith, but other faith traditions, and will incorporate studies which evidence the retention – by adolescent and adult offspring – of values, attitudes, beliefs and practices associated with the parents' faith.[35] The literature review in Chapter 3 therefore forms the backbone of this report.

Overall, what this report will do is to re-engage with the discussion around the role and responsibility of parents in the spiritual nurture of their child, and re-emphasise the significant contribution that they make to the process, and success, of passing on faith.

references – introduction

1   http://www.mumsnet.com/education/school-gate/features/tips-for-teaching-road-safety

2   Chris J Boyatzis, 'The Nature and Functions of Religion and Spirituality in Children', in KI Pargament (ed.), *APA Handbook of Psychology, Religion, and Spirituality: Volume 1: Context, Theory and Research* (Washington: American Psychological Association, 2013) pp. 497-512. In this chapter, the following definitions are adopted: "*Religion* or *religiousness* refer to institutional practices, beliefs, and experiences centering around the sacred and to the psychological functions of such practices, beliefs, and experiences. Spiritual and spirituality are used to refer to feelings, experiences, practices, and relationships with what one considers self-transcendent and sacred, which may or may not be grounded in institutional religion" (p. 497).

3   Chris J Boyatzis, 'INTRODUCTION: Advancing Our Understanding of Religious Dynamics in the Family and Parent—Child Relationship', The International Journal for the Psychology of Religion 16 (4) (2006), pp. 245-251, p. 245.

4   Boyatzis, 'Nature', p. 497; David Hay and Rebecca Nye, *The Spirit of the Child* (London: Fount, 1998).

5   Justin L Barrett, *Born Believers: The Science of Children's Religious Belief* (London: Free Press, 2013).

6   AC Grayling, *The God Argument: The Case against Religion and for Humanism* (London: Bloomsbury, 2013), p.39.

7   Justin L Barrett, 'Let's Stick to the Science', *The Guardian* 29 November 2008, http://www.theguardian.com/commentisfree/2008/nov/29/religion-children

8   Ralph W Hood Jr, Peter C Hill and Bernard Spilka, T*he Psychology of Religion: An Empirical Approach* (4th ed.) (London: Guilford Press, 2009) pp. 76, 77.

9   James Fowler, *Stages of Faith: The Psychology of Human Development and the Quest for Meaning* (New York: HarperCollins, 1981).

10 Lawrence O Richards, *Children's Ministry: Nurturing Faith within the Family of God* (Grand Rapids: Zondervan, 1983), p. 180. Richards points out that in addition to cognitive development, behavioural scientists use theories of social development and moral development in establishing a 'developmental framework' for nurturing faith (p. 14).

11 Jocelyn Bryan, 'Being and Becoming: Adolescence', in A Shier-Jones (ed.), *Children of God: Towards a Theology of Childhood* (Werrington: Epworth, 2007), pp. 135-157.

12 Francis Bridger, *Children Finding Faith* (London: Scripture Union, 1988), p. 15.

13 Hood, *Psychology*, p. 89.

14 Richard Dawkins, 'Don't Force Your Religious Opinions on Your Child', 19 February 2015, https://richarddawkins.net/2015/02/dont-force-your-religious-opinions-on-your-children

15 Grayling, *God*, p. 13.

16   Herbert Anderson and Susan BW Johnson, *Regarding Children: A New Respect of Childhood and Families* (Louisville: John Knox Press, 1994), p. 66.

17   Nick Spencer, Gillian Madden, Clare Purtill and Joseph Ewing, *Religion and Well-Being: Assessing the Evidence* (London: Theos, 2016).

18   Annette Mahoney and Annemarie Cano, 'Introduction to the Special Section on Religion and Spirituality in Family Life: Pathways between Relational Spirituality, Family Relationships and Personal Well-Being', *Journal of Family Psychology* 28 (6) (2014), pp. 735-738.

19   Michael E McCullough and Evan C. Carter, 'Religion, Self-Control, and Self-Regulation: How and why are they related?', in KI Pargament (ed.), *APA Handbook of Psychology, Religion and Spirituality: Volume 1 Context, Theory and Research* (Washington, DC: American Psychological Association, 2013), pp. 123-138.

20   Jill W Sinha, Ram A Cnaan, Richard J Gelles, 'Adolescent Risk Behaviors and Religion: Findings from a National Study', *Journal of Adolescence* 30 (2007), pp. 231-249.

21   Melissa Soenke, Mark J Landau, and Jeff Greenberg, 'Sacred Armor: Religion's Role as a Buffer against the Anxieties of Life and the Fear of Death', in KI Pargament (ed.), *APA Handbook of Psychology, Religion and Spirituality: Volume 1 Context, Theory and Research* (Washington, DC: American Psychological Association, 2013), pp. 105-122.

22   Gene H Brody, Zolinda Stoneman and Douglas Flor, 'Parental Religiosity, Family Processes, and Youth Competence in Rural, Two-Parent African American Families', *Developmental Psychology* 32 (4) (1996), pp. 696-706; Annette Mahoney, 'Religion and Families, 1999-2009: A Relational Spirituality Framework', *Journal of Marriage and Family* 72 (2010), pp. 805-827.

23   The Woolf Institute, *Report of the Commission on Religion and Belief in Public Life. Living with Difference: Community, Diversity and the Common Good* (Cambridge: The Woolf Institute, 2015), p.16. https://corablivingwithdifference.files.wordpress.com/2015/12/living-with-difference-online.pdf

24   David Voas and Laura Watt, *The Church Growth Research Programme Report on Strands 1 and 2: Numerical Change in Church Attendance: National, Local and Individual Factors* (2014) http://www.churchgrowthresearch.org.uk/UserFiles/File/Reports/Report_Strands_1_2_rev2.pdf

25   David Voas and Alasdair Crockett, 'Religion in Britain: Neither Believing nor Belonging', *Sociology* 39 (1) (2005), pp. 11-28.

26   Voas and Watt, *Church*, p. 2.

27   S Collins-Mayo, 'The Meaning and Inheritance of Anglican Identity amongst Young People', Abby Day (ed.), *Contemporary Issues in the Worldwide Anglican Communion* (Farnham: Ashgate, 2016), pp. 21-37, p. 21.

28   *Church Times*, 'Church contains hardly any converts, report suggests', 27 May 2016. https://www.churchtimes.co.uk/articles/2016/27-may/news/uk/church-contains-hardly-any-converts-report-suggests.

29   See, for example, Steve Bruce and Tony Glendinning, 'When was Secularization? Dating the Decline of the British Churches and Locating its Cause', *The British Journal of Sociology* 61 (1) (2010), pp. 107-126.

30   See 'Charting Decline – Counting the Missing' in the Introduction to Leslie J Francis and Philip
      Richter, *Gone for Good? Church-Leaving and Returning in the 21st Century* (Peterborough:
      Epworth, 2007), p. 6.

31   Grace Davie, *Religion in Britain since 1945: Believing without Belonging* (Oxford: Blackwell,
      1994).

32   Diana R Garland, 'Faith Narratives of Congregants and their Families', *Review of Religious
      Research* 44 (1) (2002), pp. 68-92.

33   Elisabeth Arweck and Eleanor Nesbitt, 'Young People in Mixed Faith Families: A Case of
      Knowledge and Experience of Two Traditions?', in M Guest and E Arweck (eds.), *Religion and
      Knowledge: Sociological Perspectives* (Farnham: Ashgate, 2012), pp. 57-75.

34   Mathew Guest, 'The Reproduction and Transmission of Religion', in PB Clarke (ed.), *The Oxford
      Handbook of the Sociology of Religion* (Oxford: OUP, 2009), pp. 651-670.

35   This report will not aim to provide a detailed philosophical or theological defence of faith
      nurture within the family, or offer a detailed account of the spiritual development and
      nurture of the child. Nor will it present a socio-political critique of the role of the family in the
      current framework of religious socialisation in the UK. This is notwithstanding the fact that all
      of these themes are relevant to the wider public debate around the nurturing of faith in the
      family, and will inevitably feature in the discussion.

religion and youth: a failure in transmission?

introduction

Every generation finds itself in unique and unscripted contexts, contexts in which the essentials of faith must be appropriated and passed on. With this in mind, the challenge of passing on faith in this era is, arguably, no different than any previous one. Yet the plurality of competing worldviews in today's cultural context, and their instant availability to children and young people, creates uncharted territory for inhabiting and narrating faith. Alongside this, signs of increased hostility towards religious worldviews would suggest that today's parents face distinct challenges in passing on faith.

In this chapter we will give attention, in particular, to the evolving association that young people are having with religion. In doing so, the following questions are worthy of our consideration: In view of the perceived decline in religiosity in the West, is religion, as some would suggest, inevitably on the way out? If so, do parents still have any effective influence in passing on faith? If they do, how are they exercising it, and what are the outcomes for young people?

In light of our discussion, we will suggest that young people's religious association and involvement is changing, yet parents and the family clearly continue to have a significant influence on the young person's sense of religious belonging. Question marks arise instead over how big a priority the passing on of faith is for parents and what essentially is being passed on.

distinct within a generation

Research indicates that young people in modern Western societies are less religious than the previous generations.[1] Naturally this finding is determined by how religiosity or 'keeping the faith' is understood – whether, for example, through church membership or attendance, or continued affiliation with parents' beliefs and values. This in turn informs how we assess successful 'passing on' or retention of faith.[2]

The British Social Attitudes Survey for 2012 found that "65% of 18-24 year olds do not affiliate to a religion, compared with 55% of the same age group (18-27) in 1983."[3] If measured within the Christian faith in terms of church membership and activity then this generational shift in the UK is particularly noteworthy within the mainstream denominations.[4]

> 65% of 18-24 year olds do not affiliate to a religion, compared with 55% of the same age group (18-27) in 1983.

Headlines have previously suggested that the Church of England, for example, is "one generation from extinction".[5] As such, so-called Generation A (Anglican laywomen born in the 1920s and 1930s) is described as the "final active generation": "The matriarch is disappearing and her children are not replacing her."[6] In light of this numerical trend, concern is understandably expressed over the future maintenance, growth and influence of the Church. Nonetheless, this is accompanied by warnings from within the denomination against adopting an unsound 'decline theology', recognising instead the Mission Action Plans and growth strategies already in place, which include a particular focus on discipling under-25s.[7]

Yet faced with these apparent trends in young people's religiosity, sociologists and, of course, church leaders are interested in finding out more about the causes and the consequences of disaffiliation. Questions invariably arise over the process of religious transmission – the 'how', 'what' and 'where' of passing on faith – and the social factors that influence and shape the cultural landscape in which faith is nurtured.

In considering these questions, the discussion in this chapter will point to research that has been done to assess the religious beliefs and practices of young people in the West. The studies identified largely represent young people from within the Christian tradition, but not exclusively. In noting observed changes to young people's values and attitudes towards religion, we will more specifically assess whether there has been an actual or perceived change in the role and influence of the home in passing on faith.

Rather than a discourse of extinction, we will propose instead that what is more apparent is a shift in young people's religious beliefs and practices. This suggests a Christian faith in the West that will be more distinct within a generation.

reasons for generational shift

There are a number of possible reasons given for the shift in young people's religiosity.[8] Firstly, there is the suggestion that religiosity is determined by the stage of life an individual is at, i.e. young people are not so much losing their religion as much as having not yet found it, or found that they needed it. In measuring religious growth and decline, the social indicator of age is recognised to have by far the strongest association with religious commitment.[9] Perhaps it has always been the case that older people are more religious than younger people.[10]

> Perhaps it has always been the case that older people are more religious than younger people.

Religiosity is indeed found to change over the life course. For example, significant life events such as marriage, parenthood, and retirement are observed to impact religiosity.[11] Also, the 'instability' of religious involvement in adolescence is seen as a cause of religious decline, with this instability continuing into emerging adulthood.[12] However, the correlation of religiosity with particular life stages is not consistently evidenced. The long-running longitudinal study, carried out by the Institute of Human Development (IHD) at the University of California, Berkeley, tracked the religious beliefs and practices of almost 200 individuals over 60 years, and found a 'gentle ebb and flow' of religiosity, with peaks in adolescence and early and late adulthood.[13] The study did, however, confirm a peak in religiosity that accompanied parenthood.

Further to the hypothesis concerned with stage of life, the decline in young people's religiosity is explained by the fact that it is an inevitable consequence of secularisation, or an indication that young people are simply experiencing and relating to religion and the sacred differently. On the first point, a correlation is drawn between religious decline and the process of modernisation within Western society. The so-called 'secularization thesis' contends that the social significance of religion, and in particular Christianity, in the Western world, will decline as societies modernise.[14] Individual freedom and consumer choice have replaced the social norms and expectations that accompanied Christian belief and association.[15]

Yet in the face of this perceived trend towards secularity, a decline in church membership does not necessarily equate with a loss of faith, nor does a decline in religious affiliation equate with a fall in identification with the spiritual. Recently published research

> A decline in church membership does not necessarily equate with a loss of faith.

investigating the reasons for a decline in attendance within the Church of Scotland reveals that two-thirds of church-leavers, despite being absent from the pews, maintain a strong personal faith.[16] In addition, results from a YouGov study in 2013 found that a quarter of respondents said they were spiritual but not religious.[17]

Thus, the stage of life thesis and the apparent trend towards secularity offer inconclusive reasons for this shift in young people's religiosity.

the priority of transmission?

Another reason given for the decline in young people's religiosity is that the older generation has failed to effectively pass on faith. Clearly a motivation and purpose for doing so is needed, at least if parents want to be intentional about the process. In line with this reason, a fall in young people's religiosity may be an indication of a problem in transmission rather than a lack of retention. Young people, as a result, may be less religious than the older generation, not because of a value shift in the importance they place on religion, but on the value and importance that their parents and family have placed on passing it on.[18]

To illustrate the point, the European Values Survey presented respondents with a list of 11 qualities that children can be encouraged to learn at home – good manners; independence; hard work; feeling of responsibility; imagination; tolerance and respect for other people; thrift, saving money and things; determination, perseverance; religious faith; unselfishness; obedience. Of the 505 self-declared Anglican respondents, only 11% listed religious faith as a priority, compared to 94% identifying good manners. While this figure may be open to the criticism of nominalism, the same criticism cannot be levelled of the fact that only 36% of those who said that their religion was very important to them listed religious faith as a priority.[19]

Further to this, research carried out by YouGov for Bible Society in 2014 found that biblical literacy was declining through the generations in Britain. Of note among the findings was the evident neglect among Christian parents to pass on the Biblical story. According to the research, almost a third (30%) of Christian parents say

Almost a third (30%) of Christian parents say that they never read Bible stories to their children.

that they never read Bible stories to their children. Furthermore 7% do not think that their child, aged over 3, has ever read, seen or heard any Bible stories. In stark contrast, 86% of parents read, listened to or watched Bible stories themselves as a child aged 3 to 16.[20]

Thus, in accounting for the change in young people's religious involvement over time, it is suggested that "parental values have become more liberal or relativistic, so that transmitting religion no longer seems critically important". In addition, "parents have become less committed to conformity in their children".[21]

The value placed on a young person's autonomy is one reason given for failing to prioritise religious transmission. This is in line with what is noted to be a distinct feature of religion, indeed of life, in modern Britain, namely a culture shift from obligation to choice.[22] This emphasis on autonomy and choice gives young people, for example, the option of not attending church.[23] Indeed, one might go further than this, to say that attending church is not only one option among many for young people, but is often treated with such derision and disdain in much mainstream culture as to tilt the choice *away* from serious religious commitment.

An evidenced lack of priority given to religious transmission, at least within the Christian home, is of particular importance for this report. For apart from all other factors in the home that might contribute to successful religious retention, re-invigorating parents' motivation and desire to pass on the Christian faith would, in the first instance, seem an obvious place to start in addressing this generational shift.

religion, young people and the family

As we question the continued place and importance of the family in religious transmission, a closer look at studies concerned with young people and religion over the past few decades will allow for a more detailed examination of these generational shifts.[24]

young people in England

Results from *The Faith of Generation Y Study*,[25] a five-year study carried out among over 300 young people attending Christian youth and community projects in England, found that young people were relating to, and practicing faith differently from the previous generation: "Young people have not inherited the rebellious hostility to the Church of their parents' generation, although for many of them religion is irrelevant for day-to-day living".[26]

Among those who identified as Anglican (just under half of the young people in the survey), around a third rarely or never went to church.[27] Yet their self-identified association with the Christian faith, its beliefs and values, was still in evidence – while just over half described themselves as being 'neither spiritual nor religious', three-quarters said that they prayed at least once a month. The same number believed that Jesus was the Son of God.[28] Sylvia Collins-Mayo, one of the authors of the report, described the "tentative nature" of their affiliation, suggesting that Christian identity was perhaps a convenient solution to questions concerned with religious association, as well as a means of distancing oneself from other faith traditions.[29]

While religious affiliation appeared tentative, 'family faith', and the sense of belonging that accompanied it, seemed to anchor young people in the tradition of their parents. As a result, many were choosing to stay within the family fold.[30] In particular, an association was drawn between their own Christian identity and a sense of belonging that came from their family narrative, for example, the significance they placed on their own christening.

Abby Day's 'believing in belonging' thesis would support this finding – belief is not confined to god or religion, but is more often located in, and reinforced by, close and trusted relationships.[31] As such, this study would suggest that young people continue to draw a positive association between faith, family life and their own religious identity: "for most young people faith is located primarily in family, friends and their selves as individuals – defined as 'immanent faith'".[32]

A further small-scale study of 40 young people (13-15 year olds) in the North of England confirmed the strength of this family association. The study, among mostly Christians and Muslim young people, noted the positive contribution that religious parents were perceived to make to the moral framework and spiritual identity of the family. This was done alongside creating an atmosphere of warmth and support in the home.[33]

> An evidenced lack of participation among young people raises concerns about the depth of commitment and the formation and nurturing of belief.

Yet despite this on-going tentative affiliation – strengthened and affirmed by a sense of relational belonging – an evidenced lack of participation among young people raises concerns about the depth of commitment and the formation and nurturing of belief.

The lack of child churchgoing is problematic because if a religious identity is to develop into something personal and meaningful beyond socially ascribed affiliations, young people need to engage with a worshipping community.[34]

This includes acquiring a personal knowledge of the objective content of the faith.

Indeed, research among young Anglican males showed that increased levels of practice, i.e. church attendance, affected religious, social and personal values.[35] Research carried out among Christian university students in England also found that "the more Christians are engaged in relational communities of faith, the more likely they are to be socially conservative, doctrinally orthodox and active citizens through volunteering."[36]

While young people have clearly not abandoned their association with the faith of their parents, concern over their current practice and engagement would appear justified in light of the solidifying influence that this has on faith formation.

young people in the US

Comparable findings to those in the UK can be found in Christian Smith's *Soul Searching: The Religious and Spiritual Lives of American Teenagers*.[37] The results of the *National Study of Youth and Religion (NSYR)* found that whilst young people were "confused and inarticulate about religion", most *"chose* to remain in general conformity with the values of their parents".[38] Indeed, Smith and Denton noted the on-going influence of parents to be a key finding of the large-scale study:

> For better or worse, most parents in fact still do profoundly influence their adolescents – often more than do their peers – their children's apparent resistance and lack of appreciation notwithstanding. This influence often also includes parental influence in adolescents' religious and spiritual lives. Simply by living and interacting with their children, most parents establish expectations, define normalcy, model life practices, set boundaries and make demands – all of which cannot help but influence teenagers, for good or ill.[39]

As an inevitable outcome of the process of socialisation, young people were largely perceived to reflect the religiosity of their parents. The impact of this process could be tracked from the adolescent years into emerging adulthood, demonstrated in the follow-up research carried out among the respondents to the *Soul Searching* study.[40]

However, the limits to this intergenerational continuity were also noted:

> It appears that parents were successful in transmitting a sense of the significance and authenticity of their religious tradition, but were less so in communicating the precise meaning of its various core doctrines and practices.[41]

Instead, the US teenagers, both religious and non-religious, were noted instead for adopting the "de facto creed" of "Moralistic Therapeutic Deism".[42]

This outlook is reflective of wider social influences and ideologies at work, such as individual self-fulfilment and consumer choice. But for our own study what it does demonstrate is that while the young people appeared to be "exceedingly conventional" in seemingly believing what they were raised to believe, Smith and Denton described an attitude towards religion that was perceived to be a background presence rather than an active, pervasive or prescriptive influence.[43] Further research among emerging adults in the US would suggest that a more "individualized" faith has emerged.[44]

Alongside the UK and the US, an emerging religious culture is also evidenced in the beliefs and values of 'Generation Y' in Australia. Research has found a decline in young people's commitment to the denomination they were raised in. In addition, only half of the respondents believed in God. Yet these findings were not distinctive of this generation, but reflected the strength of belief among the respondents' parents.[45]

conclusion

The evidence presented in this chapter would indicate that young people in the Western world appear to be relating to faith differently from previous generations. This includes a much more tentative affiliation to the beliefs and practices of their parents' religious tradition.

Young people in the Western world appear to be relating to faith differently from previous generations.

While the "passivity of so-called 'believers'" – a passivity evidenced in the fall of practices such as church attendance – is regarded as a sign of religious decline,[46] it yet appears that a more substantive shift has taken place in how faith is perceived and understood. Smith, in noting the "parasitic" effects of belief systems such as Moral Therapeutic Deism, suggests that a process of "internal secularization" has taken place within religious communities in the US, a process in which religious beliefs and practices are being fundamentally distorted.[47] For example, an individualistic, self-fulfilling vision of religious commitment has emerged, more akin to the American dream than to the cost of discipleship.

What comes more into question therefore is the content of the religious knowledge, and nature of the practices, that are being acquired: "What 'spiritual capital', then, do young people inherit today?"[48]

The shifts evidenced in this chapter raise particular challenges for passing on the historical religious traditions in a meaningful, faithful and coherent way – a challenge that parents, as we shall see in the following chapter, are ideally positioned to meet.

references – chapter 1

1   Sylvia Collins-Mayo, 'Introduction', in S Collins-Mayo and P Dandelion (eds.), *Religion and Youth* (Farnham: Ashgate, 2010), pp. 1-6.

2   Leslie Francis and Gemma Penny highlight the different understandings of religiousness or religiosity in the literature – 'believing without belonging'; 'belonging without believing '; 'believing in belonging'; 'neither believing nor belonging' ('Belonging without Practising: Exploring the Religious, Social and Personal Significance of Anglican Identities among Adolescent Males', in A Day (ed.) *Contemporary Issues in the Worldwide Anglican Communion* (Farnham: Ashgate, 2016), pp. 55-71).

3   British Social Attitudes 28, 'Religion', 2012, p. 182. http://www.bsa.natcen.ac.uk/media/38966/bsa28-full-report.pdf

4   The British Social Attitudes Survey (2014) evidenced a significant decline in the percentage self-identifying as Anglican – 40 per cent in 1983 down to 17 per cent in 2014. http://www.natcen.ac.uk/news-media/press-releases/2015/may/british-social-attitudes-church-of-england-decline-has-accelerated-in-past-decade/
Graeme Thompson offers a detailed account of young people leaving the Presbyterian Church in Northern Ireland – a reduction of 58.9 per cent in 50 years (up to the year 2010) in those becoming communicant members, in *Keeping Close to Home: The Faith and Retention of Presbyterian Emerging Adult in Northern Ireland*, Unpublished PhD Thesis (London: King's College, 2012). Overall, from 2005 to 2010 the percentage of the population in the UK who were church members fell from 12.3 per cent to 11.2 per cent. It was predicted to reach 10.3 per cent of the population by 2015, and 9.4 per cent in 2020 if trends continued (Peter Brierley, (ed.), *UK Church Statistics 2005-2015* (Tonbridge: ADBD Publishers, 2011), p. 2).

5   *Independent*, 'Church of England "one generation away from extinction" after dramatic loss of followers', 1 June, 2015. http://www.independent.co.uk/news/uk/church-of-england-one-generation-away-from-extinction-after-dramatic-loss-of-followers-10288179.html

6   Abby Day, 'Farewell to Generation A: The Final "Active Generation" in the Anglican Communion', in A Day (ed.), *Contemporary Issues in the Worldwide Anglican Communion* (Farnham: Ashgate, 2016), p. 17.

7   David Goodhew and Bob Jackson, 'Can we Grow? Yes We Can', in *How Healthy is the C of E?* (London: Canterbury Press, 2014), pp. 122-126.

8   Collins-Mayo, 'Introduction', pp. 1, 2.

9   David Voas, 'Explaining Change over Time in Religious Involvement', in S Collins-Mayo and P Dandelion (eds.), *Religion and Youth* (Farnham: Ashgate, 2010), pp. 25-32.

10 Davie, Religion, p. 121.

11 Keith A Roberts and David Yamane, *Religion in Sociological Perspective* (5th ed.) (London: SAGE, 2012), p. 97.

12 Roberts and Yamane, *Religion*, pp. 98, 99.

13   Michele Dillon and Paul Wink, *In the Course of a Lifetime: Tracing Religious Belief, Practice, and Change* (London: University of California Press, 2007).

14   Sylvia Collins-Mayo, 'Secularization and Desecularization in Europe and North America', in D Patte (ed.), *The Cambridge Dictionary of Christianity* (Cambridge: Cambridge University Press, 2010), pp. 1139-1142. She notes that "the 'loss of social significance' is taken to mean both a decline in the power and influence religion has over social organization, and the decreasing salience, plausibility, and usefulness of traditional religious beliefs and practices for the majority of people in their daily lives" (p. 1140).

15   Collins-Mayo, 'Meaning'.

16   The Church of Scotland, 'New research reveals Britain's Christian community considerably larger than expected', 24 March 2016. http://www.churchofscotland.org.uk/news_and_events/news/recent/new_research_reveals_britains_christian_community_considerably_larger_than_expected

17   Woolf, *Commission*, p. 18.

18   Voas, 'Explaining', p. 29.

19   Voas and Watt, 'Church', p. 18.

20   Bible Society, *'Pass it On'* Research Report, February 2014, p. 22.

21   Voas, 'Explaining', p. 29.

22   Davie, *Religion*, p. 4.

23   Voas, 'Explaining', p. 29.

24   Andrew Singleton offers a helpful overview of large-scale national studies that offer significant insight into religion and youth in contemporary society: The *National Study of Youth and Religion* (NSYR) in the United States, the *Spirit of Generation Y* (SGY) study in Australia, the *Teenage Religion and Values Survey* (TRVS) in England and Wales, *Project Teen Canada* (and previous national level data collected by Reg Bibby), and the *Young Melanesian Project* (YMP) in Papua New Guinea. This is not, notes Singleton, to negate the usefulness of smaller-scale projects (*Religion, Culture and Society: A Global Approach*, (London: SAGE, 2014)).

25   Sylvia Collins-Mayo, Bob Mayo, Sally Nash and Christopher Cocksworth, *The Faith of Generation Y*, (London: Church House Publishing, 2010). Note: 'Generation Y' refers to the generation born in the 1980s and 1990s.

26   The Church of England, 'Generation Y has a faint cultural memory of Christianity but is not hostile towards religion, five-year study reveals', 4 October 2010. https://www.churchofengland.org/media-centre/news/2010/10/pr8610.aspx

27   Collins-Mayo, 'Meaning', p. 26.

28   *Ibid.*

29   *Ibid.*, p. 28.

30   *Ibid.*, p.30.

31   Abby Day, '"Believing in Belonging": An Exploration of Young People's Social Contexts and Constructions of Belief', in S. Collins-Mayo and P. Dandelion (eds.), *Religion and Youth*, (Farnham: Ashgate, 2010), pp. 97-103.

32   The Church of England, 'Generation Y'.

33   Janet Lees and Jan Horwath, '"Religious Parents… Just Want the Best for Their Kids": Young People's Perspectives on the Influence of Religious Beliefs on Parenting', *Children & Society*, 23, (2009), pp. 162–175.

34   Collins-Mayo, 'Meaning', p. 31.

35   Francis and Penny, 'Belonging', pp. 55-71.

36   Mathew Guest, Kristen Aune, Sonya Sharma and Rob Warner, *Christianity and the University Experience: Understanding Student Faith* (London: Bloomsbury Academic, 2013), p. 197.

37   Christian Smith and Melinda L. Denton, *Soul Searching: The Religious and Spiritual Lives of American Teenagers* (New York: OUP, 2005).

38   Guest, 'Reproduction', pp. 662, 663. Emphasis original.

39   Smith and Denton, *Soul*, p. 56.

40   Christian Smith and Patricia Snell, *Souls in Transition: The Religious and Spiritual Lives of Emerging Adults* (Oxford: OUP, 2009).

41   Guest, 'Reproduction', p. 663.

42   "The creed of this religion, as codified from what emerged from our interviews, sounds something like this:
      1.   A God exists who created and orders the world and watches over human life on earth.
      2.   God wants people to be good, nice, and fair to each other, as taught in the Bible and by most world religions.
      3.   The central goal of life is to be happy and to feel good about oneself.
      4.   God does not need to be particularly involved in one's life except when God is needed to resolve a problem.
      5.   Good people go to heaven when they die."
      Smith and Denton, *Soul*, pp. 162, 163.

43   Ibid., p. 120.

44   Jeffrey Jensen Arnett and Lene Arnett Jensen, 'A Congregation of One: Individualized Beliefs Among Emerging Adults', *Journal of Adolescent Research*, 17 (5) (2002), pp. 451-467.

45   Michael Mason, Andrew Singleton and Ruth Webber, *The Spirit of Generation Y: Young People's Spirituality in a Changing Australia* (Mulgrave: John Garret, 2007), p. 96.

46   Voas and Crockett, 'Religion', p. 24.

47   Christian Smith, 'Is Moral Therapeutic Deism the New Religion of American Youth? Implications for the Challenge of Religious Socialization and Reproduction', in James L Heft, SM (ed.), *Passing on the Faith: Transforming Traditions for the Next Generation of Jews, Christians, and Muslims* (New York: Fordham University Press, 2006), pp. 55-74.

48   Collins-Mayo, 'Introduction', pp. 1, 2.

faith in the family: how it is passed on

introduction

At the outset of this report, we alluded to some of the culturally shaped roles and responsibilities associated with contemporary parenting. In particular, we questioned whether the spiritual nurture of the child fitted into this matrix. Studies exploring the religious and spiritual lives of young people affirm that parents play a key role in faith development, not least in creating a sense of religious belonging. However, studies have also given rise to questions concerning the substantive content of young people's religious beliefs and practices.

Our discussion in this chapter will give further attention to how parents and the family are understood as agents in the process of passing on faith. In addition, we will identify the importance of religious teaching and tradition in informing the content of the process. This will lead us in the following chapter to note, in particular, what characteristics of family life are found to make a difference in this process.

What will become increasingly evident in this report is that the social context of the family matters – and matters significantly – for shaping the religious beliefs and practices of the child and emerging adult.

The social context of the family matters – and matters significantly – for shaping the religious beliefs and practices of the child and emerging adult.

learning faith in the home

The interactions of family life understandably engage the interest of those who want to understand how faith transmission works, and, if possible, why adolescent and adult offspring do, or do not, continue in the faith tradition of their parents. Philip Richter and Leslie Francis, reporting on their research findings amongst church leavers in England and Wales,[1] suggest that the "foundations of church going, or church leaving, are laid in a person's childhood, during his or her most formative years".[2] The religious socialisation that takes place in the home, they suggest, is of primary importance. "Even if religion in contemporary society is, to a considerable extent, a matter of individual consumer choice, religious choices are heavily influenced by religious consumption patterns laid down early in life."[3]

As such, sociologists make the case for the relationship between parents' beliefs and practices and the future religious orientation of their child. This positive correlation applies to parents who associate with a religious tradition and those who do not. Research carried out among atheists in the US, for example, evidenced that 30% had at least one atheistic parent, while many others were raised in homes with little interest in religion.[4]

In engaging with the process of socialisation, we are concerned with how beliefs and values are passed on to the next generation. Attention is directed in particular to the major agents of socialisation – "parents and the family, congregations and religious education, peers and schools".[5] In doing so, a distinction is drawn between the *microsystems* that influence a child's development (family, school, peer group, religious community) and the *macrosystems* that are part of the wider context of socialisation (cultural values and ideologies). We are primarily concerned in this report with the microsystem of the family, and the pre-eminent influence it exercises.[6]

Parents remain the primary agents for the transmission of beliefs and behaviours.[7] The Woolf Institute *Report on Religion and Belief in Public Life* noted that religion "can be determined – partly, largely or even entirely – by the family and community into which a person is born, and by how they are perceived and treated by others."[8] Incorporated into this observation is the implicit overlap of ethnicity and religion and the importance of family identity. In addition to their direct influence, parents can also indirectly influence the other *microsystems* of socialisation, including those of peers and the religiosity of the school.[9]

> The social learning of religion in the family is done through "spiritual modelling" and the "observational learning" that accompanies it.

The social learning of religion in the family is done through "spiritual modelling" and the "observational learning" that accompanies it. The observation and imitation of parents' beliefs and behaviours both positively reinforces the desired religious beliefs and practices and negatively reinforces the unwanted ones.[10]

More specifically, the Social Learning Theory points to four main processes that direct observational learning and influence effective modelling: *Attention* (paying attention to particular information or behaviour), *Retention* (remembering what has been seen), *Reproduction* (replicating it),[11] and *Motivation* (having motivation and a reason to replicate it). These processes can encourage spiritual engagement and growth – *attention* can be directed to key figures of the faith through the reading of Scripture, while *retention* is encouraged through the repeated reading of Scripture; virtues of the faith are modelled in religious communities and *reproduced*, and *motivation* is received in and through the regular opportunities to meet for mutual encouragement.[12]

From these processes, we can see that spiritual modelling encompasses behaviours, skills, and attitudes. It is a way to actively facilitate the transmission of faith. In addition, the social learning of religion can be both proactive and passive: the former involves a direct or conscious strategy to pass on religious knowledge, whereas the latter involves learning by experience and doing, where knowledge is absorbed and embodied.[13] In other words, 'spiritual modelling' can aid spiritual growth and faith transmission. However, if the transmission of faith in the home is unintentional or undirected, it will happen anyway due to our social nature and interactions.

> If the transmission of faith in the home is unintentional or undirected, it will happen anyway due to our social nature and interactions.

It is important to note that parents are not excluded from the outcomes of this process of faith transmission.[14] A "transactional model" of socialisation highlights the fact that there is a two-way exchange that takes place, where parents are also shaped in the process. In addition, parental spiritual formation within a larger community is also deemed an essential part of the spiritual nurture of children.[15]

In sum, alongside the 'preparedness' hypothesis, which advocates a child's propensity to understand and engage with religious ideas, theories of religious socialisation point to the influence of the family in shaping the future religiosity of adolescents and adults. This is done both passively and actively, and includes observation and imitation, where beliefs, values and behaviours are learnt, integrated and maintained. The spiritual nature of the child is thus shaped by the spiritual nurture it receives. In addition, "this natural tendency is enhanced when parents and others reinforce this with explicit religious instruction."[16]

religious tradition and transmission

We have given particular attention so far to the 'how' of faith transmission in the home. Yet faith transmission and formation in the home is shaped by the tradition in which it takes place. Understanding the role of the family cannot overlook the cultural, ethnic and religious contexts in which the family is located. For some religions – Judaism and Hinduism, for example – culture and faith are 'intimately intertwined'. For others, Protestant Christianity being the obvious example, the association is somewhat less obvious.[17] Arguably, Christianity, in all its traditions, is influenced by the culture in which it finds itself. In the African diaspora Christian communities in Britain, for example, where religion is more than just a set of beliefs, faith is intimately connected to the socio-political issues that affect the community and shape identity.[18] Assessing successful faith transmission needs to take account of the diversity of these contexts and traditions.

The family is encouraged to provide the context for a 'critical education' which allows for, critical reflection of the faith tradition.

When it comes to the Christian community, the nurture and transmission of faith is shaped by a theological understanding of the child. Discussion across the Christian tradition is infused with the theological question over whether the aim of children's ministry is conversion or nurture.[19] Yet even within a single denomination, different constructs of childhood are evident.[20] Despite these differences, parenting and family life are regarded as central to the nurture and development of the child, and as means of spiritual development and formation.[21] The family is also encouraged to provide the context for a 'critical education' which allows for, and facilitates, critical reflection of the faith tradition.[22] There is no shortage of resources on how this spiritual nurture might be translated from a theological premise to a practical reality.

Transmission within other religious traditions will clearly be shaped by different teachings and practices. Britain is noted for the diversity of 'world religions' that now co-exist,[23] and recent research enables us to glimpse the processes of faith transmission within a few of these traditions.

A research project among young British Sikhs, for example, has revealed a large diversity of religious knowledge and practice between families. This is influenced by caste and migration history, which shapes the degree to which the knowledge and practises of Sikhism are learned and adopted, for example gurdwara attendance, knowledge of Sikh history, speaking the Punjabi language and visiting the Punjab. The structure of the family, and in particular the accessibility of grandparents, also positively impacts religious socialisation.

Muslims are almost twice as likely to report practicing the same religion they were brought up in.

Muslims form the largest non-Christian religious minority in Britain and their numbers continue to increase.[25] The BSA survey in 2014 indicated a ten-fold rise in Islam, from around half a percent of the population in 1983 to around five per cent in 2014.[26] Evidence would suggest that the level of faith retention in British Muslim communities is high. *Muslim Childhood: Religious Nurture in a European Context*, a detailed qualitative research report carried out among 60 Muslim families in Cardiff, was an attempt to explore why Muslims are almost twice as likely to report practicing the same religion they were brought up in.[27]

The report identified the foundations of nurture and education, including the central role of the family in Islamic law and teaching, highlighting the belief that while everyone is born a Muslim, the flourishing of faith is dependent on family upbringing, the wider social context, and education:

> Islamic sources outline in detail the mutual obligations of parents and children towards one another, including the parental responsibility for the religious nurture and education of children. A saying of the Prophet Muhammad, often quoted by Muslims, reads: "A father gives his child nothing better than a good education."[28]

The research also emphasised the importance of the family's role in the continuity of tradition and practice, with, for example, almost all families questioned arranging for their children to learn the Qur'an in Arabic.[29] Indeed, religious habits and family practices can be seen to accord with theories of religious socialisation. The frequent repetition of Quranic phrases and the religious activity of parents and grandparents, such as prayer, are seen to contribute to successful transmission. In the collective practice of religious rituals, Muslim homes "become permeated by religious observance."[30]

For many British Muslims, religion comes before ethnicity and indeed all other identity markers, suggesting a 'Muslim first' association. In addition, an individuated spirituality, which is observed within the Western context, does not accord with the collective nature and practice of Islam.[31] The family is affirmed in religious teaching, and remains central in religious education and practice. "British Muslims recognize the critical importance of a strong family life and effective education for the future transmission of Islam."[32]

Clearly social learning plays a key role in faith transmission in the home, and is particularly effective when accompanied by clear conviction and content, as the above examples suggest.

conclusion

In this chapter we have presented a brief synopsis of the theory behind the social learning of faith that takes place in the home. In addition to that, we have highlighted the importance of the religious cultures and traditions that give these practices shape and meaning. Alongside a short account of how religious nurture is understood in the

Christian tradition, we have also taken account of the role and purpose of the family in religious transmission among Sikhs and Muslims in Britain.

So much more could be said on all accounts. Yet the main purpose of our discussion in this chapter is to emphasise the on-going influence of parents and the family in religious transmission, and to highlight the potential, as well as the inevitable, socialisation that takes place within these familial relationships.

In light of this, the following conclusion from Smith's US study of teens is not an inevitable but a very plausible outcome of this modelling and learning:

> By normal processes of socialization, and unless other significant forces intervene, more than what parents might *say* they *want* as religious outcomes in their children, most parents most likely will end up getting religiously of their children what they themselves *are*.[33]

The evidence presented in the next chapter will demonstrate that this assertion rings true in many homes.

references – chapter 2

1   Philip Richter and Leslie J Francis, *Gone but not Forgotten: Church Leaving and Returning* (London: Darton, Longman and Todd, 1998); LJ Francis and P Richter, *Gone for Good? Church-leaving and Returning in the 21st Century* (Peterborough: Epworth, 2007).

2   Richter and Francis, *Gone*, p. 77.

3   *Ibid.*

4   Bruce E Hunsberger and Bob Altemeyer, *Atheists: A Groundbreaking Study of America's Nonbelievers* (New York: Prometheus Books, 2006), p. 42.

5   Roberts and Yamane, *Religion*, p. 95.

6   Boyatzis, 'Nature', p. 502.

7   Roberts and Yamane, *Religion*, p. 95.

8   The Woolf Institute, *Report*, p. 15.

9   Roberts and Yamane, *Religion*, p. 97.

10 *Ibid.*

11 Doug Oman, 'Spiritual Modeling and the Social Learning of Spirituality and Religion', in KI Pargament (ed.), *APA Handbook of Psychology, Religion, and Spirituality, Volume 1: Context, Theory and Research* (Washington, DC: American Psychological Association, 2013), pp. 187-204.

12 Oman, 'Spiritual', pp. 189, 190.

13 Arweck and Nesbitt, 'Young'.

14 Jan Horwath, Janet Lees and Peter Sidebotham, 'The Influence of Religion on Adolescent Family Life in England: An Explanatory Study of Views of Young People and Parents', *Social Compass*, 59 (2) (2012), pp. 257-275. See also 'Children in the Family', in S May, B Posterski, C Stonehouse and L Cannell, *Children Matter: Celebrating their Place in the Church, Family and Community* (Grand Rapids: Michigan, 2005).

15 Catherine Stonehouse, *Joining Children on the Spiritual Journey: Nurturing a Life of Faith* (Grand Rapids: Baker Books, 1998), p. 64.

16 Hood, Hill and Spilka, *Psychology*, p. 90.

17 Elisabeth Arweck and Eleanor Nesbitt, 'Young People's Identity Formation in Mixed-Faith Families: Continuity or Discontinuity of Religious Traditions?', *Journal of Contemporary Religion*, 25 (1) (2010), pp. 67-87.

18 Interview with Professor Robert Beckford, Professor of Theology and Culture in the African Diaspora. Carried out on 11 May 2016 at Canterbury Christ Church University.

19 Bridger, *Children*, p. 132. Howard Worsley helpfully traces and summarises these theological positions – one focussing on 'Original Blessing', the other on 'Original Sin' (see Howard Worsley, 'Conversion: A New Paradigm', *Childrenswork Magazine*, 1 (14) October 2014, pp. 22-25).

20   See, for example, Anna Strhan, 'Evangelical Anglicans and the Formation of Children in Modern Britain', in A Day (ed.), *Contemporary Issues in the Worldwide Anglican Communion* (Farnham: Ashgate, 2016), pp. 39-53.

21   See, for example, Ray S Anderson and Dennis B Guernsey, *On Being Family: A Social Theology of the Family*, (Grand Rapids: WB Eerdmans, 1985).

22   See, for example, Jeff Astley, 'The Role of the Family in the Formation and Criticism of Faith', SC Barton (ed.), *The Family: In Theological Perspective*, (Edinburgh: T&T Clarke, 1996), pp. 187-202.

23   Grace Davie, *Religion in Britain: A Persistent Paradox (2nd ed.)*, (Oxford: Wiley Blackwell, 2015), p. 59.

24   Jasjit Singh, 'Keeping the Faith: Reflections on Religious Nurture among young British Sikhs', *Journal of Beliefs & Values*, 33 (3) (2012), pp. 369-383.

25   Davie, Religion in Britain: *A Persistent Paradox*, p. 61.

26   Ruth Gledhill, 'Church of England decline accelerates, while other faiths grow', *Christianity Today*, 2015. http://www.christiantoday.com/article/church.of.england.decline.accelerates. while.other.faiths.grow/55050.htm

27   Jonathan Scourfield, Sophie Gilliat-Ray, Asma Khan and Sameh Otri, *Muslim Childhood: Religious Nurture in a European Context* (Oxford: OUP, 2013), p. 43.

28   Scourfield et al., *Muslim*, pp. 21, 22.

29   *Ibid.*, p. 77.

30   Sophie Gilliat-Ray, *Muslims in Britain: An Introduction* (Cambridge: CUP, 2010), p. 139.

31   Jonathan Scourfield, Rosalind Warden, Sophie Gilliat-Ray, Asma Khan and Sameh Otri, 'Religious Nurture in British Muslim Families: Implications for Social Work', *International Social Work*, 56 (3) (2013), pp. 326-342.

32   Gilliat-Ray, *Muslims*, p. 130.

33   Smith and Denton, *Soul*, p. 57.

passing on family faith: what makes a difference?

introduction

We have so far affirmed in this report that parents remain key players in the religious socialisation of their children. This is not just an assumption of social theory, but has been affirmed through the self-reported experience of a significant number of young people. Parents should have confidence, therefore, in the continued strength of the role that they play in nurturing the spiritual nature and developing faith of their children.

This is not to detract from the motivation and responsibility for passing on faith that emanates from religious teaching and traditions. It simply recognises the fact that in a complex world of competing social influences and ideas, parents remain highly effective in passing on faith. This is the case whether they intend to be or not.

In a complex world of competing social influences and ideas, parents remain highly effective in passing on faith.

Building on these findings, this final chapter aims to bring together research that points to factors within family life that make a difference to passing on faith – i.e. factors that aid or hinder adolescent or adult offspring successfully retaining the religious beliefs and practices of their parents. Studies will be categorised under three headings: *relational*, *behavioural*, and *structural*, and the key findings from each study will be presented.

the science of 'keeping the faith'

Investigating the successful passing on of faith in the home is a scientific endeavour – it does not ask the normative questions of what should be done, but instead it observes and measures the outcomes of what is done. Like any scientific endeavour, it does this through proposing hypotheses, collecting data, and analysing findings. For the social scientist, therefore, questions for clarification arise, such as how religiosity will be measured and how successful transmission or retention will be assessed.

There is not a straightforward, 'one size fits all' approach to undertaking this type of investigation. Leslie Francis and Philip Richter, for example, explore the challenges of defining the concept of 'church-leaver' due to the multiple ways of defining religiosity, including affiliation, belief, membership or practice. They note that research literature has tended to focus on practice, observed through church attendance, as a marker of religiosity, though this is not without its conceptual and practical challenges, i.e. what level and type of practice equates with high-level religiosity.[1]

As noted already, undoubtedly the danger exists in any empirical study of religion that the richness of the subject matter is reduced to a mere scientific investigation. In doing so, we lose the meaning, complexity and variety of the human experience that is being analysed.[2] In light of this, it is rightly judged 'problematic' that in the past three decades more than three quarters of studies on religion and family have measured religiosity using only one or two items.[3] Both individual religiosity and faith practices within the family are invariably more complex; they cannot be sufficiently assessed by, for example, the frequency of parental and adolescent church attendance or the regularity of Bible reading.

Further limits on measuring religiosity and religious transmission in the family should also be noted. While some studies will offer only a one-time measurement of the religious affiliation, beliefs and practices of parents and their children, others will observe how beliefs and practice change at different intervals over the life-course. It is suggested that multiple survey items are in fact needed – concerned with identity, practice and belief – in order to give a reliable picture of faith commitment.[4] In addition, the family offers only one among multiple cultural and social variables that might influence and shape religious formation.

> Knowing what potentially makes a difference to outcomes can better inform practices.

Nevertheless, we will proceed on the assumption that the scientific study of 'keeping the faith' is a fruitful endeavour in so far as knowing what potentially makes a difference to outcomes can better inform practices. It also has the potential to identify beliefs and practices that are at odds with the teaching and traditions of a faith.

measuring faith retention in the home

Researchers have adopted a number of different approaches to assessing the influence of parents in passing on faith. These include: simple measures of 'keeping the faith' – a child identifying with the family faith as they grow up; measuring attitudinal agreement between the parent and the child on religious matters; and the self-reported influence that a child or young person attributes to their parents. Some studies, for example, have asked adolescent or adult offspring to consider what impact they feel their parents have had on their own beliefs and practices.[5]

In developing these approaches – as we will see in the reports that follow – researchers have identified not only the religious 'experience'[6] that is passed on, e.g. church attendance, but the factors in the home that correlate with the success, or indeed failure, of the transmission of this experience, e.g. the nature of the relationship with the father. Thus, a hypothesis to be tested might look something like this: 'A warm and supportive relationship with the father relates positively to a young person's church attendance'.

Three characteristics of parenting and family life are found in the research literature to influence the outcomes of faith transmission: *the quality of relationships*, including the parent-child relationship and the relationship between the parents; *unity of traditions*, i.e. parents who come from the same religious tradition or reflect the same level of religious commitment; and *stability of family structure*, i.e. children growing up in families that are 'intact'.[7] In addition to these, empirical research on religious transmission also correlates the type of relationship (i.e. whether the child's relationship is with father/mother/ grandparent), the style of parenting, and the religious behaviour of parents, with the future religiosity of the child.

> Three characteristics of parenting and family life are found in the research literature to influence the outcomes of faith transmission: the quality of relationships, unity of traditions, and stability of family structure.

The studies in this chapter will be categorised under three headings: *relational*, *behavioural*, and *structural*.

- The relational category will incorporate studies that highlight both the type of family relationship and the quality of the relationship.

- The behavioural category will include studies that identify as significant the style of parenting as well as the religious practice of the parents.

- The structural category will summarise studies that point to both the importance of a unity of traditions in the home, i.e. parents coming from the same religious tradition and reflecting the same religious commitment, as well as studies that point to the significance of the stability of the family structure, including the strength of the marital relationship, and families that remain 'intact'.

Individual studies may well fit into more than one category. Studies will also adopt different measures of religious experience which will influence how religious retention is understood.[8]

relational factors

In the studies that follow we will note, in particular, the type of familial relationships and the nature of those relationships that are significant for faith transmission. This includes relationships with the mother, father, grandparents and siblings. Studies also measure how the quality of these relationships are perceived and reported.

type of relationship

Bengtson et al. (2013)[9] published results from a large-scale longitudinal study in the US, collecting survey data from 3,500 parents, grandparents, grandchildren and great-grandchildren over a 35 year period (1970-2005). From an analysis of the survey data they identified factors that appeared to encourage or hinder faith transmission. One such factor, which they noted to be 'crucial', was the quality of the parent-child relationship:

> When children perceive their relationship with parents as close, affirming, and accepting, they are most likely to identify with their parents' religious practices and beliefs, while relationships marked by coldness, ambivalence, or preoccupation are likely to result in religious differences. (p. 98)

The father's piety on its own was not sufficient in encouraging religious transmission, but needed to be accompanied by emotional warmth.

In particular, within certain faith traditions the perceived emotional closeness with the father mattered more than emotional closeness with the mother.[10] This was particularly of note among the evangelical participants. Thus, a significant finding from the study was that the father's piety on its own was not sufficient in encouraging religious transmission, but needed to be accompanied by emotional warmth.

An earlier finding from Bengtson's research noted the relationship with the mother as a significant predictor of religious transmission. Acock and Bengston (1978), in research carried out among 653 father-mother-youth triads, highlighted the greater influence of the mother than of the father on the child's political and religious socialisation. Various variables concerned with behaviours, attitudes and beliefs were used to measure the similarity between young adults (16-26 year olds) and their parents. Particular similarity was noted when it came to religious behaviour, supporting the importance placed on the effect of social modelling that takes place in the home:

> In short, contrary to much previous commentary and research, mothers are more predictive of the child's orientations than are fathers. The only exception is with respect to Religious Behavior. On Religiosity, Tolerance, and Sexual Norms, fathers' scores are slightly more predictive than mothers. (p. 225)

Another US-based, father-mother-youth triad study conducted by Dudley and Dudley (1986) measured the agreement on religious value statements from 712 individual surveys within Seventh-day Adventist congregations. The study evidenced a stronger correlation between young people and mothers than between young people and fathers.

An adolescent's perception of a parent's acceptance is also a predictor of religious outcomes. Bao et al. (1999), reporting on findings from a sample of 407 families living in rural Iowa, found that the importance of the mother's perceived warmth and acceptance was particularly important for sons and correlated with successful religious transmission.

An adolescent's perception of a parent's acceptance is also a predictor of religious outcomes.

Beyond the father and mother, research also points to the significance of the extended family and the role that it plays in successful religious transmission. Bengtson et al. (2013) noted the 'unexpected importance of grandparents', reflective of the lack of attention they have received in understanding religious socialisation. Drawing on the Longitudinal Study of Generations (LSOG) across generations from 1971-2000, Bengston et al. (2009) used grandparent–parent–grandchild triads (257 grandparents, 341 parents, 565 grandchildren) to examine the transmission of three dimensions of religiosity – religious service attendance, religiousness and religious ideology. They noted how both parents and grandparents operated simultaneously as independent *and* joint agents of religious socialisation, highlighting the particular influence of grandmothers on granddaughters.

Research also points to the significance of the extended family and the role that it plays in successful religious transmission.

Copen and Silverstein (2007), using the same sample but asking further questions of it, also noted that religious socialisation was strengthened when mothers and grandmothers shared strong religious beliefs. However, while affirming this correlation, they also noted their sample was limited due to its regional nature (majority of respondents in Southern California) and its social and ethnic bias (affluent, non-Hispanic). Similar to other reports based on survey data, a lack of detailed observation of the transmission process, including an understanding of not just the direct but the indirect means of religious transmission, places limitations on the findings.

In addition to the influence of parents and grandparents, Gutierrez et al. (2014) extended the scope of familial relationships and considered the positive influence of siblings on an adult's religiosity and values. The study, carried out among African American families, concluded the following:

> Of the 320 participants, only 1% indicated mother, 7% father, 2% grandmother, 2% grandfather, 2% brother(s), and 2% for sister(s) as having negatively affected one's religiosity or spirituality. These data suggest that, within and across generations, fathers are most likely to have a negative influence, but that family members, on the whole, rarely have an adverse effect on religious socialization. (p. 781)

Therefore, while again the study was limited by sample size, and geographical and ethnic specificity, it highlighted the importance of recognising the potential influence of significant familial relationships.

quality of the parent-child relationship

Research noted already has pointed to the perceived warmth of the father and acceptance of the mother as correlating with higher levels of religious transmission. The following reports explore further the *quality* of the relational dynamics within the home. These include studies that have attempted to assess the effect of early childhood experiences – in particular, the security of the parent-child relationship – on future beliefs and practices. Two hypotheses have been presented, which draw an association between childhood attachment and religiosity.

The first, the 'compensation hypothesis', predicts that people who have not had secure relationships with their parents will be inclined to compensate this with belief in God and religion.[11] Kirkpatrick and Shaver (1990) proposed and partially supported this hypothesis in their own research, although among their 213 respondents, it only held when parents themselves were relatively non-religious. The second, the 'correspondence hypothesis', suggests that a secure childhood attachment corresponds with successful socialisation.[12]

Research conducted among university students in Sweden offered support for both hypotheses (Granqvist, 1998; Granqvist and Hagekull, 1999; Granqvist, 2002). Results of questionnaires carried out among 203 students, measuring the quality of their childhood attachment along with their own and their parents' religiosity "supported the compensation hypothesis in that insecure respondents, to a larger extent than secure respondents, reported an increase in importance of their religious beliefs during adulthood" (Granqvist, 1998, p. 350). However, the correspondence hypothesis was also evidenced, where secure respondents with highly religious parents demonstrated a greater adoption of religious standards than insecure respondents (Granqvist and Hagekull, 1999).

Alongside these findings, there was a noted difference between the two groups of respondents. For the secure respondents (associated with the correspondence hypothesis) there were found to be smaller fluctuations in religious beliefs and behaviours compared to the insecure respondents (associated with the compensation hypothesis). The latter were noted for their unstable religiosity (Granqvist, 2002, p. 266). Therefore, early childhood attachment theories and related research do appear to point to the importance of the security of the parent-child relationships in determining the future religiosity of the child, in particular, the future stability of religious beliefs.

Despite these findings, questions nevertheless arise as to whether a reliable correlation can be drawn between the self-reported influence that young adults place on their childhood experiences and their current religiosity. Hoge et al. (1993) at least noted the potential weakness of data results when adult respondents are recalling back 20 to 30 years. The results of their own research, measuring the membership and attendance of young adults in the Presbyterian Church in the US, found that early experiences were not strongly associated with current church involvement, including the parent-child bond. The religious beliefs of the young adults, and their current family relationships and concerns, were a greater determinant of present church involvement. This would indicate that perhaps the impact of early religious socialisation diminishes with age, and the strength of later influences increases. Nevertheless, early experiences were significant in that they predicted religious beliefs, which in turn influenced church involvement.

In an earlier study, Hoge et al. (1982), using 254 mother-father-youth triads within Catholic, Baptist, and Methodist churches in the US, measured the effect of 33 family factors on the transmission of religious and social values. While most had no effect, several factors were noted to enhance religious value transmission – "younger age of parents, parental agreement about religion, and good parent-child relationships" (p. 569).

In addition to emotional security, emotional support has been shown to correlate with positive consensus between parent-child religious experiences. In a study among 125 Jewish adolescents and their fathers, Herzbrun (1993) noted that among traditional fathers and their sons, the father's emotional support correlated with strong religious consensus. The same correlation was not observed among liberal fathers; the author suggests that perhaps in these cases the emotional support was perceived to be more unconditional. However, with daughters, the emotional support of the liberal father did make a difference on the outcome of the parent-child consensus.

In a study carried out among daughters at a Midwestern University in the US, the perceived warmth of the parent-child relationship was noted to correlate positively with the child's perception of their parents' beliefs. Okagaki and Bevis (1999), in the study among 62 young women and their parents, noted that the accuracy of the daughters' perception was also related to how frequently parents talked about their beliefs and to the agreement between the mother and father on those beliefs. Daughters who perceived that the beliefs were important to their parents were more likely to adopt those beliefs.

In measuring changes in religious affiliation over a seven year period, closeness to parents prevented apostasy and switching religions.

Sherkat and Wilson (1995), at the University of Michigan, also concluded that feelings of closeness to parents had an influence on religious choices. In measuring changes in religious affiliation over a seven year period, closeness to parents prevented apostasy and switching religions. So did patterns of attendance laid down in youth. "Parents influence their children's preferences both directly and by getting them to attend church, and these preferences in turn drive their children's religious choices as adults" (p. 1015).

Despite the lack of detailed observations of faith practices in the home, there is some research that points to relational practices that make a difference. Flor and Knapp (2001), for example, noted the positive correlation between higher levels of parent-child communication and future religiosity. In a study involving 171 two-parent families with an early adolescent, the following conclusion was drawn: "As mother- and father-child discussions of faith became more frequent and bidirectional, both adolescents' religious behaviour and the importance they attached to religion increased" (p. 642).

The quality of the interaction also makes a difference. In data from 223 British adolescent-mother pairs, Taris and Semin (1997) found the quality of the interaction between the mother and the young person influenced the successful transmission of religious values. High quality interactions were those that were marked by a parent's "openness, affection and accessibility" (p. 213).

This leads us on to our second category of research – that which identifies the importance of the behaviour of parents, including the parenting style adopted and the patterns of religious practice in the home.

behavioural factors

Parenting practices have important implications for a child's development. This is a well-established and proven theory of developmental psychology. Religious orientation and commitments will also have an influence on parenting style and practices. However, limited research has been done on the implications of parenting style for religious development.[13]

parenting style

Approaches to parenting can be determined by religious conviction, where religious teaching and tradition inform how parents undertake the task. In turn, different styles of parenting are found to impact and influence adolescent development and behaviour, including their religious development. While authoritarian parents are demanding and generally unresponsive, with a strong emphasis on rules and obedience, authoritative parents are demanding yet responsive, open to explaining rules and exploring their child's perspective.[14] Danso et al. (1997) highlight the implications of a right-wing authoritarian style of parenting, linked to religious fundamentalism, on the practices of parenting, for example, with an emphasis on obedience over autonomy. Research suggests that the authoritative style is more beneficial for a child's development, including their religious development.

Abar et al. (2009) found that authoritative parenting, unlike authoritarian or permissive parenting, facilitated the transmission of religious values among African-American young people. Levels of religiosity were higher among students who had experienced this style of parenting. Conversely, Luft and Sorell (1987) noted that where parenting was "low in control and low in nurturance" there was less creedal and value consensus between parent and adolescent (p. 53). Permissive and inattentive parenting, this research would suggest, are not conducive to passing on faith.

> Authoritative parenting, unlike authoritarian or permissive parenting, facilitated the transmission of religious values among African-American young people.

At the same time, the importance and impact of parental control on faith transmission appears to be age-specific. Potvin and Sloane (1985) pointed to other variables, including the religious experience and the age of the adolescent, when noting the effectiveness of parental control.

At early ages parental control and personal religious experience are compatible and their combination produces high levels of religious practice. At later ages, however, they are incompatible and high religious experience is associated with higher practice only when parental control is low. (p. 12)

This suggests that maintaining high levels of parental control as the child gets older can be detrimental to continued religious practice.

The quality of the parent-child relationship, and the integrity and consistency of the parent's own religious practice, continue to be strong determinants of successful religious transmission.

Dudley (1978), in researching the impact of 'fundamentalist religious homes' among 400 Seventh-day Adventist adolescents, also noted the importance of the relationship with parents and the consistency of belief and practice among those in authority. Further, Dudley and Wisbey (2000) found that parenting style in early childhood, as recalled by Seventh-day Adventist young adult respondents in the US and Canada, influenced the level of commitment to the Church:

For this sample of young adults, the parenting style most conducive to encouraging youth to remain in the church as enthusiastic members was a mixture of loving care and protection or control. The most ineffective style was the control without the loving care. Thus affection and care appear to be the active ingredients in a parenting style that leads to positive relationships with the church in future years. (p. 49)

Parenting style clearly has the potential to impact the future religiosity of a child. However, the quality of the parent-child relationship, and, as we will come on to discuss, the integrity and consistency of the parent's own religious practice, continue to be strong determinants of successful religious transmission.

belief and religious practice

A significant number of studies point to the correlation between the religiosity of parents and the successful transmission of religion. This includes the importance of parents practicing what they preach. Religious practices, initiated in the home, influence adolescent and adult religious beliefs and practices, as the following studies evidence.

As noted earlier, individual research studies cannot always be categorised tidily under one of our three headings. Myers (1996), for example, indicated three variables in the family context that affected religious transmission: "parental religiosity, quality of the family relationship, and traditional family structure". These are in line with our own three categories – behavioural, relational and structural. The study among 471 parents and their adult offspring concluded that religiosity of adults was "determined largely by the religiosity of one's parents" (p. 858).

Research has found that young adults who recall a greater emphasis on religion in the home appear to be more religious. Hunsberger (1976), in a questionnaire among 457 students at the University of Manitoba in Western Canada, concluded that the "greater perceived emphasis parents placed on religion as their children were growing up was related to the agreement of university students with their parent's religious teaching" (p. 254). This finding was confirmed in a later study among 875 students at the University of New South Wales in Sydney, Australia. Hunsberger and Brown (1984) noted in their findings that

> respondents with the stronger emphasis placed on religion in their childhood home were more likely to remain within their childhood religious 'umbrella', while those who reported a weaker emphasis were more likely to become apostates. (p. 250)

Regnerus and Uecker (2006), in their investigation of the social context in which adolescent religiosity develops, noted that parental religious service attendance was the strongest factor in shaping how important religion was in adolescents. Practices also shape attitudes towards religion. Kay and Francis (1996) drew together a range of studies conducted over a twenty-five year period, which assessed attitudes to Christianity during childhood and adolescence. In examining the influence of the home on the formation of a positive attitude towards Christianity, one significant factor was the religious example of the parents, including the importance of parental church attendance:

> Clearly the formation of attitudes within the life of the child is an internal and unobservable process. Nevertheless, these findings have shown that church attendance, whether by the child or the parents, helps a positive attitude toward Christianity to be formed. (p.70)

The significance of religious practices within the home is also noted. McNamara et al. (2013) measured the relation between faith activities in the home during childhood and adolescence and the religious beliefs and practices of emerging adults. They noted that both the frequency and importance of these activities positively impacted the emerging adults' beliefs and practices, in particular, among women, Caucasians, and Protestants. The researchers acknowledged that more work could be done in identifying which activities in particular make a difference.

Religious transmission is higher when parents' attitudes match their behaviour and practice. Consistency is key.

The importance of the consistency of parents' attitudes, beliefs and actions is also noted. Bader and Desmond (2006) examined a nationwide (US) sample of young people and their parents (approx. 2,800), from a variety of Protestant groups, as well as Catholics, Jews and other religious affiliations. Their results indicate that religious transmission is higher when parents' attitudes match their behaviour and practice. Consistency is key. "For all outcome measures, children of consistently religious parents displayed higher levels of religiosity than children raised by religiously inconsistent parents" (p. 326). This includes consistency between the religious beliefs of parents.

Earlier we noted the warmth of the father-child relationship in fostering religious transmission. Some studies also indicate the importance of the father's religiosity. Baker-Sperry (2001), in a survey among 1,058 self-identified Catholics in the US, noted that the most important finding in the study was the significance of the father's religiosity for religious transmission. The influence of the father was equal to the mother, if not stronger. Measures of religiosity among parents included frequency of mass attendance and frequency of Bible reading.

Studies have also set out to measure whether the relationship between parental religious activity and adolescent religious activity is gender specific. Kieren and Munro (1987), in their Canadian-based study of 235 intact families with adolescents, noted that the father's religious activity was 'significantly related' to the adolescent daughter's religious activity. Nelsen (1980), on the other hand, in data from 2,734 adolescents in intact families in Southern Minnesota, noted that the mother's religiosity particularly impacted sons. Kay and Francis (1996), in their synthesis of studies, drew a correlation between the father and the son, while Francis and Gibson (1993) noted that the mother's religious practice was a more powerful predictor among both sons and daughters than the father's practice. In light of these findings, there is not conclusive evidence of a gender specific parental effect on an adolescent's religious experience.

A higher level of parental religiosity leads to stronger family relationships and better outcomes for young people.

Research also indicates that a higher level of parental religiosity leads to stronger family relationships and better outcomes for young people. Brody et al. (1996) found that "greater formal religiosity is related directly to more cohesive family relationships, lower levels of interparental conflict, and fewer externalizing and internalizing problems among young adolescents" (p. 703).

Thus, while adolescents are likely to "revise their religious beliefs" in the process of their development, Ozorak (1989) suggests that the religiosity of parents is "a stabilizing factor, particularly if they belong to a faith with a strong group identity and they are emotionally close to the adolescent" (p.451). The parents' faith acts as a "cognitive anchor", particularly among early and middle adolescents. In a small-scale study among emerging adults in the Presbyterian Church in Ireland, Thompson (2012) also found this to be the case:

> Those who said either parent had an outstanding or strong and open faith also appear more likely to be involved in church and have a more active faith, but those whose parents were less expressive of their faith seem to have experienced a more negative impact on their faith and church attendance. (p. 217)

Studies have also assessed the significance of the parents' beliefs and practice compared to other social variables, for example, youth groups, Sunday schools, and peer groups. Parker and Gaier (1980), in examining the relationship between religious beliefs and religious practices of 46 members of a Conservative Jewish youth group, assessed the effect of different variables: "Sex, Hebrew School Background, number of years of affiliation with the group, and parental practices." Only the final variable, the practices of parents, was statistically significant. While not dismissing the importance of religious education outside of the home, the study concluded:

> Religious Belief Systems are formed at home. If one wants to affect the values of the child, he must first affect those of the parents, whereby the parent should become active in the religious education of his child. (p. 372)

Regnerus et al. (2004), in assessing the role of the multiple social and religious contexts (parents, friends, school, extended community) in the development of adolescent religiosity, noted that parents and friends strongly influenced the church attendance of the adolescents questioned in the nation-wide (US) longitudinal study. Out of the social variables measured, it was the churchgoing habits of the parents that were noted to have the strongest influence on the churchgoing habits of the adolescent. Further, Regnerus and Uecker (2006) confirmed the importance of religious context (religiosity of schoolmates and parents) for the future religiosity of adolescents: "families where parents are high in religiosity seem to foster in adolescent children a rapid growth in religious salience and (especially) attendance, as well as to prevent rapid loss of either form of religiosity" (p. 229).

Schwartz (2006) also found that the religious modelling of parents, alongside that of friends, significantly influenced adolescents' religious faith. The strength of this influence can also be noted by its duration. Martin et al. (2013) found parental influence and that of peers did not change throughout the adolescent years. However, among adult offspring, Poch and Hastings (1998) observed that the effect of parental attendance on adult participants' church attendance was still significant, but not more so than the effect of other variables, including marital status and the presence of children. Salience of religion (membership of a religious organisation) was noted to be the variable with the most powerful effect. As such, for adult offspring, the current social context, including church friendship groups, may arguably be more important for maintaining church involvement than parental beliefs and practices.

structural factors

We have noted that the type and quality of the parent-child relationship impacts on religious transmission. Added to this, the beliefs and practices of the parents have a strong predictive effect on the beliefs and practices of the adolescent. Finally, a correlation is drawn between the stability of the parental relationship – including a unity of beliefs and values, and the stability of the family structure – with the future religiosity of the child.

unity of parental beliefs and values

On the question of parental unity of beliefs and values – in terms of what this contributes to parental stability and thus wider family stability, and in turn to the effective passing on of faith – research suggests that active religious transmission is not prioritised within mixed-faith families. Data from a three-year ethnographic study (2006–2009) at the University of Warwick, which investigated the identity formation of young people in mixed-faith families (Christian, Hindu, Muslim and Sikh), concluded that transmitting the actual content of religion, beyond the identification of universal values, was of little importance to parents (Arweck and Nesbitt, 2010a). In their findings, Arweck and Nesbitt (2010b) observed that the parents in question were not themselves committed believers and, not wanting to impose a particular tradition on the child, they "tend to want their children to have at least the option of becoming part of a religious tradition, whether it is their own or a different one" (p. 84).

Mixed-faith marriage is positively associated with religious disaffiliation.

Research points to the fact that mixed-faith marriage is positively associated with religious disaffiliation. Sandomirsky and Wilson (1990) confirmed their hypothesis that "children of religiously mixed marriages will have higher apostasy rates than children of religiously homogenous marriages" (p. 1215). Unity of faith practices positively influences transmission. Voas and Storm (2012), in a study of intergenerational churchgoing in England and Australia, found that the "impact of two churchgoing parents on their children is considerably stronger than that of one alone" (p. 393). Such findings appear to justify the assertion that "religiously mixed marriages tend to undermine religious involvement."[15]

Petts and Knoester (2007) also found that in families where there is significant religious difference between parents, there are lower levels of religious participation. This, they suggest, may have negative implications for a child's wellbeing, based on the evidence that religion benefits families, e.g. strengthening of intra-family bonds. Bartkowski et al. (2008) also found that shared faith commitments between parents can positively contribute to a child's development, whereas conflict over religion is detrimental: "religion can serve as a bridge that links generations and yields pro-social outcomes, but can also function as a wedge that fosters division and conflict, thereby undermining children's development" (p. 33).

quality and stability of marital relationship

When it comes to factors concerned with the internal structure of the family, research indicates that the quality of the marital relationship positively contributes to the religious beliefs and practices of adolescents. Day et al. (2009) assessed the association between both the quality of the parental marital relationship, and the parent-adolescent relationship, with the religiosity of the adolescent. On both accounts they noted that the closeness and the quality of the relationship made a significant contribution to the strength of adolescent religious conviction and practice. This causal link would suggest that, "where there is more interpersonal stability, there is a greater likelihood that desired goals, aspirations, dreams, and personal beliefs are easier to transfer" (p. 307).

Poor parental marital relationships also affect religious socialisation in the longer-term.

Poor parental marital relationships also affect religious socialisation in the longer-term. Myers (1996), in addition to his conclusion on the importance of parents' religiosity, found that those raised by both biological parents, with a high level of marital happiness, were more likely to continue religious practice into adulthood. This is compared to those from single-parent households or raised in step-families. The structure and stability of the family context contributes to "religiosity inheritance". In measuring religiosity in terms of religious salience and attendance, Regnerus and Uecker (2006) also observed the impact of family structure on, in particular, religious decline: "biologically intact two-parent families are given to religious stability: adolescents from such families do not exhibit considerable increase in religiosity, yet are also less likely to report steep decline" (p. 231).

Such findings would imply that parental divorce is detrimental to successful faith retention. Lawton and Bures' (2001) findings suggested that this is the case. Using the data from 11,372 respondents to the National Survey of Families and Households in the US, they concluded that "for individuals raised as either moderate Protestant, conservative Protestant or Catholic, parental divorce increases the likelihood of both switching to another religion and apostasy" (p. 99). This supported the hypothesis that religious ties are weakened through divorce because of the disruption it causes to familial and communal relationships.

Zhai et al. (2007) observed the association between parental divorce and "substantially lower self-reported religious involvement" among young adults from divorced families compared with those from intact families The effects were not observed outside of organised religious activity, i.e. personal prayer life, or on the young adults' subjective religious experience, i.e. feeling close to God (p. 125). In discussing the possible reasons for this finding, the study showed that divorced fathers were much less involved in the religious socialisation of their offspring, which may have accounted for the lower attendance.

The experience of separation and divorce is not age-specific – it is felt by adolescents and young adults alike. Francis (2001), in his values survey among more than 33,000 young people between the ages of 13 and 15 in England and Wales, found that those who had experienced separation or divorce were "less inclined to subscribe to traditional Christian beliefs than young people from intact families" (p. 147). Bryant et al (2003) also found that, among first year college students, religiosity was negatively affected by those experiencing their parents' divorce. In contrast, family cohesion and spending time together as a family positively related to religious and spiritual outcomes.

conclusion

When it comes to 'passing on' and 'keeping' faith, the studies highlighted in this chapter would strongly suggest that what happens within the context of family life significantly impacts the process and outcomes of faith transmission. In drawing this conclusion, it does no harm to reinforce the point that the science of 'keeping the faith' can only tell us so much. Empirical studies will only ever be able to identify correlations rather than determine the cause of religious retention or change – assuming, indeed, that either of these can or should be 'measured'.

Nevertheless, what the research in this chapter does offer is broad observations concerned with relational dynamics and practices in the home that correlate with successful faith transmission. From the studies, we can draw out the following conclusions:

- Adolescents and young adults who experience or who have experienced close, affirming, and accepting relationships with both parents are more likely to identify with the beliefs and practices of their parents.

- The security and stability of the parent-child relationship, including the strength of the childhood attachment, informs the stability of future religious beliefs.

- The influence of grandparents, and indeed the wider family, plays a positive role in faith formation.

- Authoritative parenting – where the exercise of discipline and control is accompanied by warmth, nurture and responsiveness – is more conducive to religious transmission than authoritarian or permissive parenting.

- The consistency of parental religious practice, which includes the importance that is placed on it and the integrity with which it is exercised – both inside and outside the family home – positively correlates with the practice of adolescents and adult offspring.

- In addition, parental religiosity acts as a stabilising factor within the family unit, particularly when both parents share and practice the same faith.

- Conversely, religious ties are weakened as a result of parental disunity when it comes to faith and practice, or as a result of family instability – including the negative experience of divorce for adolescents and young adults.

Many of the above factors – emotional warmth, security, stability etc. – have an impact on a child's overall development, including their psychological, emotional and relational development. What we can note from the research in this chapter is that these factors equally have a long-lasting impact on a child's spiritual development.

Yet it is important to acknowledge that all of these factors, particularly when viewed from a theological standpoint, do not have the last word in determining spiritual outcomes. The Christian parent can at least affirm that God's grace has the first and the final word.

references – chapter 3

1   Francis and Richter, *Gone*, p. 28.

2   Hood et al., *Psychology*, p. 25.

3   Boyatzis, 'Nature', p. 504.

4   David Voas, 'Religious Involvement over the Life Course: Problems of Measurement and Classification', *Longitudinal and Life Case Studies 6* (2015), pp.212-227. Beyond social theory, research also points to, for example, the influence and importance of adolescent personality styles on future religiousness (Paul Wink, Lucia Ciciolla, Michele Dillon and Allison Tracy, 'Religiousness, Spiritual Seeking, and Personality: Findings from a Longitudinal Study', *Journal of Personality 75* (2007), pp. 1051 – 1071; David McClintock, 'Transmitting Denominational Faith. Why Jerry and Not Jane?', *Journal of Research on Christian Education 6* (1) (1997), pp. 3-19).

5   Hood et al., *Psychology*, p. 112.

6   Three domains, used in social psychology for discussing human experience, are used for measuring the complexity of the religious experience – the cognitive (how religious belief and ideas are viewed and understood), the affective or emotional (the attitudes, values and preferences associated with religious belief), and the behavioural (how people act in light of religious belief). (Hood et al., *Psychology*, p. 39).

7   Roberts and Yamane, *Religion*, pp. 95-97.

8   This report will identify the current understanding of religiosity and faith transmission within existing literature – how that is measured, and the factors that are identified as contributing to it. This is done instead of imposing our own definition or measure of success. This is particularly important on account of the fact that the review embraces literature concerned with retention across a number of religious traditions.

9   All studies will be referenced according to the name of the first author and the year of publication. The full reference will be listed in the bibliography.

10 Religious traditions represented included Evangelical Protestant, Mainline Protestant, Catholic, Mormon, Jewish, and 'None'.

11 Hood et al., *Psychology*, p. 101.

12 *Ibid*, p. 102.

13 *Ibid*, p. 90.

14 *Ibid*.

15 Voas, 'Explaining', p. 31.

conclusion

parents: an enduring influence

Raising children in a complex and rapidly changing world presents many challenges for parents, not least the challenge of articulating and passing on faith with confidence. Parents can feel disempowered and overwhelmed in the task of nurturing faith.

This could be on account of the many competing social and cultural forces at work – notably the influence of media, the pressure from peers, or the popular secular script. It could also be on account of parents' own self-imposed demands – the desire to consistently do and say the right thing and 'succeed' at religious practices in the home. This pressure is no doubt particularly felt by devout parents who simply want to do a good job of bringing their child up in the faith.

Lawrence Richards, in his theological reflections on children's ministry, notes what happens when committed Christian parents' own expectations are not met: "The gap between ideal and perceived performance often leads to a diffused sense of guilt and of failure, which seems most intense in those to whom faith is most significant."[1] The same could probably be said of devout parents from any religious tradition.

While not ignoring these challenges and pressures, the evidence in this report at least demonstrates that parents' influence on the spiritual outcomes of their children is consistently significant – not only is it foundational to faith development, but it continues to carry considerable social weight into adolescence and adulthood.

> Parents' influence on the spiritual outcomes of their children is consistently significant.

This influence should not, of course, be seen in isolation from other social factors, including the role and importance of the wider faith community in supporting and nurturing the growth of faith. Nevertheless, the social learning that takes place in the home, including the spiritual modelling of both parents, is clearly formational. The impact on beliefs and practices can be witnessed for years to come.

In effect, the research studies presented in this report show that adolescent and adult offspring who continue to identify with the faith of their parents, are more likely to be products of caring, supportive, and stable homes. These are homes in which the nurturing of faith is a priority, and where sincere and consistent beliefs and practices – both inside and outside of the home – are seen and heard.

> That adolescent and adult offspring who continue to identify with the faith of their parents, are more likely to be products of caring, supportive, and stable homes.

attentive nurturing of faith

The majority of our discussion has focussed on articulating and assessing the process of faith transmission. This is in line with the clear remit of the report, concerned primarily with identifying characteristics of parenting and family life that make a difference in successfully passing on faith. Further ethnographic studies, incorporating more detailed observations on family practices, traditions and rituals, would strengthen our understanding of this process.

Alongside reinforcing the influence of parents in faith formation and transmission, the conclusion of this report also invites questions over how that influence is being exercised, in addition to what content is being transmitted. For example, when it comes to the transmission of faith, questions arise as to what level of priority is given to doing so, by which means, and with what confidence.

These questions arise for us in view of the generational shift in religious commitment, and evidenced changes to young people's beliefs and practices – both of which have been touched on in this report.

These questions also become more urgent in view of the danger that parents adopt the false premise that a child can – or should – be brought up independent of any particular religious tradition or worldview. While an entirely 'valueless' existence is an impossibility, Christian Smith, in his US study, affirms that young people cannot have, and do not need, a completely autonomous existence:

> About the last thing today's teenagers need is to be isolated, ignored, left alone, and made autonomous.

> In fact, about the last thing today's teenagers need is to be isolated, ignored, left alone, and made autonomous. Contemporary teenagers rather desperately need – in addition to an appropriate amount of personal 'space' – connection, support, guidance, instruction, and boundaries – even as they continually renegotiate their transition away from dependence and towards interdependence with adults.[2]

This is true for their spiritual development as much as it is true for any other aspect of their personal development. Parents should be encouraged, therefore, to forge strong relationships that incorporate faith rituals, practices and conversations about religious beliefs.

Thus, when evidence emerges that faith transmission has been deprioritised in the home, or the content of faith has been distorted, a direct challenge is posed to the current community of believers. The challenge centres around what level of importance is currently given to the passing on of faith, and what effectively is being passed on.

The wider context in which faith is transmitted will inevitably change, yet the responsibility remains for all believers to attentively nurture the faith of the next generation, as they themselves duly inhabit and narrate their own. In light of this ongoing task, Smith's closing 'sociological advice' to religious educators seems particularly apt:

> [One should] stop listening so much to the advice of sociologists, psychologists, and other experts of modernity and start paying more serious attention to and develop more confidence in the historical and theological wellsprings of one's own religious faith.[3]

This may be an important and timely piece of advice for parents, and indeed all those engaged in the privileged task of passing on faith.

references – conclusion

1   Lawrence O Richards, *Children's Ministry: Nurturing Faith within the Family of God* (Grand Rapids: Zondervan, 1983), p. 186.

2   Christian Smith, 'Is Moral Therapeutic Deism the New Religion of American Youth? Implications for the Challenge of Religious Socialization and Reproduction', in James L Heft, SM (ed.), *Passing on the Faith: Transforming Traditions for the Next Generation of Jews, Christians, and Muslims* (New York: Fordham University Press, 2006), pp. 55-74, p. 59.

3   Smith, 'Moral', p. 72.

bibliography

Abar, B, Carter, KI and Winsler, A, 'The Effects of Maternal Parenting Style and Religious Commitment on Self-Regulation, Academic Achievement, and Risk Behavior among African-American Parochial College Students', *Journal of Adolescence, 32* (2) (2009), pp. 259-273.

Acock, AC and Bengston, V, 'On the Relative Influence of Mothers and Fathers: A Covariance Analysis of Political and Religious Socialization', *Journal of Marriage and Family,* 40 (3) (1978), pp. 519-530.

Anderson, RS and Guernsey, DB, *On Being Family: A Social Theology of the Family* (Grand Rapids: WB Eerdmans, 1985).

Anderson, H and Johnson, SBW, *Regarding Children: A New Respect of Childhood and Families* (Louisville: John Knox Press, 1994).

Arnett, JJ and Jensen, LA, 'A Congregation of One: Individualized Beliefs Among Emerging Adults', *Journal of Adolescent Research,* 17 (5) (2002), pp. 451-467.

Arweck, E and Nesbitt, E, 'Close Encounters? The Intersection of Faith and Ethnicity in Mixed-Faith Families', *Journal of Beliefs and Values: Studies in Religion and Education, 31* (1) (2010a), pp. 39-52.

Arweck, E and Nesbitt, E, 'Young People's Identity Formation in Mixed-Faith Families: Continuity or Discontinuity of Religious Traditions?', *Journal of Contemporary Religion,* 25 (1) (2010b), pp. 67-87.

Arweck, E and Nesbitt, E, 'Young People in Mixed Faith Families: A Case of Knowledge and Experience of Two Traditions? in M Guest and E Arweck (eds.), *Religion and Knowledge: Sociological Perspective* (Farnham: Ashgate, 2012), pp. 57-75.

Astley, J, 'The Role of the Family in the Formation and Criticism of Faith' in SC Barton (ed.), *The Family: In Theological Perspective* (Edinburgh: T&T Clarke, 1996), pp. 187-202.

Baker-Sperry, L, 'Passing on the Faith: The Father's Role in Religious', *Sociological Focus,* 34 (2) (2001), pp. 185-198.

Bader, CD and Desmond, SA, 'Do as I Say and as I Do: The Effects of Consistent Parental Beliefs and Behaviours upon Religious Transmission', *Sociology of Religion*, 67 (3) (2006), pp. 313-329.

Barrett, J.L., 'Let's Stick to the Science', *The Guardian,* 29 November 2008, http://www.theguardian.com/commentisfree/2008/nov/29/religion-children

Bao, W-N et al., 'Perceived Parental Acceptance as a Moderator of Religious Transmission among Adolescent Boys and Girls', *Journal of Marriage and Family,* 61 (2) (1999), pp. 362-374.

Barrett, JL, *Born Believers: The Science of Children's Religious Belief* (London: Free Press, 2013).

Bartkowski, JB, Xu, X and Levin, ML, 'Religion and Child Development: Evidence from the Early Childhood Longitudinal Study', *Social Science Research*, 37 (2008), pp. 18-36.

Bengston, VL, *Families and Faith: How Religion is passed down across Generations* (New York: OUP, 2013).

Bengston, V et al., 'A Longitudinal Study of the Intergenerational Transmission of Religion', *International Sociology*, 24 (3) (2009), pp. 325-345.

Bible Society, *'Pass it On' Research Report*, February 2014.

Boyatzis, CJ, 'INTRODUCTION: Advancing Our Understanding of Religious Dynamics in the Family and Parent-Child Relationship', *The International Journal for the Psychology of Religion*, 16 (4) (2006), pp. 245-251.

Boyatzis, CJ, 'The Nature and Functions of Religion and Spirituality in Children', KI Pargament (ed.), *APA Handbook of Psychology, Religion, and Spirituality: Volume 1: Context, Theory and Research* (Washington, DC: American Psychological Association, 2013), pp. 497-512.

Bridger, F, *Children Finding Faith* (London: Scripture Union, 1988).

Brierley, P (ed.), *UK Church Statistics 2005-2015* (Tonbridge: ADBD Publishers, 2011).

British Social Attitudes 28, 'Religion', 2012 http://www.bsa.natcen.ac.uk/media/38966/bsa28-full-report.pdf

Brody, GH, Stoneman, Z and Flor, D, 'Parental Religiosity, Family Processes, and Youth Competence in Rural, Two-Parent African American Families', *Developmental Psychology*, 32 (4) (1996), pp. 696-706.

Bruce, S and Glendinning, T, 'When was Secularization? Dating the Decline of the British Churches and Locating its Cause', *The British Journal of Sociology,* 61 (1) (2010), pp. 107-126.

Bryan, J, 'Being and Becoming: Adolescence', in A Shier-Jones (ed.), *Children of God: Towards a Theology of Childhood* (Werrington: Epworth, 2007), pp. 135-157.

Bryant, AN, Choi, JY and Yasuno, M, 'Understanding the Religious and Spiritual Dimensions of Students' Lives in the First Year of College', *Journal of College Student Development*, 44 (6) (2003), pp. 723-745.

Church Times, 'Church contains hardly any converts, report suggests', 27 May 2016, https://www.churchtimes.co.uk/articles/2016/27-may/news/uk/church-contains-hardly-any-converts-report-suggests

Collins-Mayo, S, 'Introduction', in S Collins-Mayo and P Dandelion (eds.), *Religion and Youth* (Farnham: Ashgate, 2010), pp. 1-6.

Collins-Mayo, S, 'Secularization and Desecularization in Europe and North America', in D Patte (ed.), *The Cambridge Dictionary of Christianity* (Cambridge: CUP, 2010), pp. 1139-1142.

Collins-Mayo, S, 'The Meaning and Inheritance of Anglican Identity amongst Young People', Abby Day (ed.), *Contemporary Issues in the Worldwide Anglican Communion* (Farnham: Ashgate, 2016), pp. 21-37.

Collins-Mayo, S et al., *The Faith of Generation Y* (London: Church House Publishing, 2010).

Copen, C and Silverstein, M, 'Transmission of Religious Beliefs across Generations: Do Grandparents Matter?', *Journal of Comparative Family Studies*, 38 (4) (2007), pp. 497-510.

Crockett, A and Voas, D 'Generations of Decline: Religious Change in 20th Century Britain', *Journal for the Scientific Study of Religion*, 45 (4) (2006), pp. 567-584.

Danso, H, Hunsberger, B and Pratt, M, 'The Role of Parental Religious Fundamentalism and Right-Wing Authoritarianism in Child-Rearing Goals and Practices', *Journal for the Scientific Study of Religion,* 36 (4) (1997), pp. 496- 511.

Davie, G, *Religion in Britain since 1945: Believing without Belonging* (Oxford: Blackwell, 1994).

Davie, G, *Religion in Britain: A Persistent Paradox (2nd ed.)* (Oxford: Wiley Blackwell, 2015).

Dawkins, R, 'Don't Force Your Religious Opinions on Your Child', 19 February 2015, https://richarddawkins.net/2015/02/dont-force-your-religious-opinions-on-your-children

Day, A, '"Believing in Belonging": An Exploration of Young People's Social Contexts and Constructions of Belief', in S Collins-Mayo and P Dandelion (eds.), *Religion and Youth* (Farnham: Ashgate, 2010), pp. 97-103.

Day, A 'Farewell to Generation A: The Final "Active Generation" in the Anglican Communion', A Day (ed.), *Contemporary Issues in the Worldwide Anglican Communion*, (Farnham: Ashgate, 2016), pp. 3-20.

Day, RD et al. 'Family Processes and Adolescent Religiosity and Religious Practice: View From the NLSY97', *Marriage & Family Review*, 45 (2009), pp. 289–309.

Dillon, M and Wink, P, *In the Course of a Lifetime: Tracing Religious Belief, Practice, and Change* (London: University of California Press, 2007).

Dudley, RL, 'Alienation from Religion in Adolescents from Fundamentalist Religious Homes', *Journal for the Scientific Study of Religion*, 17 (4) (1978), pp. 389-398.

Dudley, RL and Dudley, MG, 'Transmission of Religious Values from Parents to Adolescents', *Review of Religious Research*, 28 (1) (1986), pp. 3-15.

Dudley, RL and Wisbey, RL, 'The Relationship of Parenting Styles to Commitment to the Church among Young Adults', *Religious Education*, 95 (1) (2000), pp. 39-49.

Flor, DL and Knapp, NF, 'Transmission and Transaction: Predicting Adolescents' Internalization of Parental Religious Values', *Journal of Family Psychology*, 15 (4) (2001), pp. 627-645.

Fowler, J, *Stages of Faith: The Psychology of Human Development and the Quest for Meaning* (New York: HarperCollins, 1981).

Francis, LJ, *The Values Debate: A Voice from the Pupils* (London: Woburn Press, 2001).

Francis, LJ and Gibson, HM, 'Parental Influence and Adolescent Religiosity: A Study of Church Attendance and Attitude towards Christianity among 11-12 and 15-16 year olds', *The International Journal for the Psychology of Religion*, 3 (4) (1993), pp. 24I-253.

Francis, LJ and Richter, P, *Gone for Good? Church-Leaving and Returning in the 21st Century* (Peterborough: Epworth, 2007).

Francis, LJ and Penny, G, 'Belonging without Practising: Exploring the Religious, Social and Personal Significance of Anglican Identities among Adolescent Males', in A Day (ed.), *Contemporary Issues in the Worldwide Anglican Communion* (Farnham: Ashgate, 2016), pp. 55-71.

Garland, DR, 'Faith Narratives of Congregants and their Families', *Review of Religious Research*, 44 (1) (2002), pp. 68-92.

Gilliat-Ray, S, *Muslims in Britain: An Introduction*, (Cambridge: CUP, 2010).

Gledhill, R, 'Church of England decline accelerates, while other faiths grow', *Christianity Today*, 31 May 2015, http://www.christiantoday.com/article/church.of.england.decline.accelerates.while.other.faiths.grow/55050.htm

Goodhew, D and Jackson, B, 'Can we Grow? Yes We Can', *How Healthy is the C of E?* (London: Canterbury Press, 2014), pp. 122-126.

Granqvist, P, 'Religiousness and Perceived Childhood Attachment: On the Question of Compensation or Correspondence', *Journal for the Scientific Study of Religion*, 37 (1998), pp. 350-367.

Granqvist, P, 'Attachment and Religiosity in Adolescence: Cross-sectional and Longitudinal Evaluations', *Personality and Social Psychology Bulletin*, 28 (2002), pp. 260-270.

Granqvist, P and Hagekull, B, 'Religiousness and Perceived Childhood Attachment: Profiling Socialized Correspondence and Emotional Compensation', *Journal for the Scientific Study of Religion*, 38 (1999), pp. 254-273.

Grayling, AC, *The God Argument: The Case against Religion and for Humanism* (London: Bloomsbury, 2013).

Guest, M, 'The Reproduction and Transmission of Religion', PB Clarke (ed.), *The Oxford Handbook of the Sociology of Religion* (Oxford: OUP, 2009), pp. 651-670.

Guest, M et al., *Christianity and the University Experience: Understanding Student Faith* (London: Bloomsbury Academic, 2013).

Gutierrez, IA et al., 'Religious Socialization in African American Families: The Relative Influence of Parents, Grandparents, and Siblings', *Journal of Family Psychology*, 28 (6) (2014), pp. 779-789.

Hay, D and Nye, R, *The Spirit of the Child* (London: Fount, 1998).

Herzbrun, M, 'Father-Adolescent Religious Consensus in the Jewish Community: A Preliminary Report', *Journal for the Scientific Study of Religion*, 32 (2) (1993), pp. 163 – 168.

Hoge, DR, Petrillo, GH, and Smith, EI, 'Transmission of Religious and Social Values from Parents to Teenage Children', *Journal of Marriage and Family*, 44 (3) (1982), pp. 596-580.

Hoge, DR, Johnson, B and Luidens, DA, 'Determinants of Church Involvement of Young Adults Who Grew up in Presbyterian Churches', *Journal for the Scientific Study of Religion*, 32 (3) (1993), pp. 242-255.

Hood, RW Jr, Hill, PC and Spilka, B, *The Psychology of Religion: An Empirical Approach (4th ed.)* (London: Guilford Press, 2009).

Horwath, J, Lees, J and Sidebotham, P, 'The Influence of Religion on Adolescent Family Life in England: An Explanatory Study of Views of Young People and Parents', *Social Compass*, 59 (2) (2012), pp. 257-275.

Hunsberger, B, 'Background Religious Denomination, Parental Emphasis, and the Religious Orientation of University Students', *Journal for the Scientific Study of Religion*, 15 (3) (1976), pp. 251- 255.

Hunsberger, B and LB Brown, 'Religious Socialization, Apostasy, and the Impact of Family Background', *Journal for the Scientific Study of Religion*, 23 (3) (1984), pp. 239-251.

Hunsberger, BE and Altemeyer, B, *Atheists: A Groundbreaking Study of America's Nonbelievers*, (New York: Prometheus Books, 2006).

The Independent, 'Church of England "one generation away from extinction" after dramatic loss of followers', 1 June 2015 http://www.independent.co.uk/news/uk/church-of-england-one-generation-away-from-extinction-after-dramatic-loss-of-followers-10288179.html

Kay, WK and Francis, LJ, *Drift from the Churches: Attitude toward Christianity during Childhood and Adolescence* (Cardiff: University of Wales, 1996).

Kieren, DK and Munro, B, 'Following the Leaders: Parents' Influence on Adolescent Religious Activity', *Journal for the Scientific Study of Religion*, 26 (2) (1987), pp. 249-255.

Kirkpatrick, LA and Shaver, PR, 'Attachment Theory and Religion: Childhood Attachments, Religious Beliefs, and Conversion', *Journal for the Scientific Study of Religion*, 29 (3) (1990), pp. 315-334.

Lawton, L and Bures, R, 'Parental Divorce and the 'Switching' of Religious Identity', *Journal for the Scientific Study of Religion*, 40 (1) (2001), pp. 99-111.

Lees, J and Horwath, J, '"Religious Parents… Just Want the Best for Their Kids": Young People's Perspectives on the Influence of Religious Beliefs on Parenting', *Children & Society*, 23 (2009), pp. 162–175.

Luft, GA and Sorell, GT, 'Parenting Style and Parent-Adolescent Religious Value Consensus', *Journal of Adolescent Research*, 2 (1987), pp. 53-68.

Mahoney, A, 'Religion and Families, 1999-2009: A Relational Spirituality Framework', *Journal of Marriage and Family*, 72 (2010), pp. 805-827.

Mahoney, A and Cano, A, 'Introduction to the Special Section on Religion and Spirituality in Family Life: Pathways between Relational Spirituality, Family Relationships and Personal Well-Being', *Journal of Family Psychology*, 28 (6) (2014), pp. 735-738.

Martin, TF, White, JM and Perlman, D, 'Religious Socialization: A Test of the Channeling Hypothesis of Parental Influence on Adolescent Faith Maturity', *Journal of Adolescent Research*, 18 (2) (2003), pp. 169-187.

Mason, M, Singleton, A and Webber, R, *The Spirit of Generation Y: Young People's Spirituality in a Changing Australia* (Mulgrave: John Garret, 2007).

May, S, Posterski, B, Stonehouse, C and Cannell, L, *Children Matter: Celebrating their Place in the Church, Family and Community* (Grand Rapids: Michigan, 2005).

McClintock, D, 'Transmitting Denominational Faith Why Jerry and Not Jane?', *Journal of Research on Christian Education*, 6 (1) (1997), pp. 3-19.

McCullough, ME and Carter, EC, 'Religion, Self-Control, and Self-Regulation: How and why are they related?', in KI Pargament (ed.), *APA Handbook of Psychology, Religion and Spirituality: Volume 1 Context, Theory and Research* (Washington, DC: American Psychological Association, 2013), pp. 123-138.

McNamara, BC, Prenoveau, JM and Diehl, CJ, 'The Value of Walking the Walk: The Relation between Family Faith Activities and Emerging Adults' Religiousness', *Journal of Psychology & Christianity*, 32 (3) (2013), pp. 206-220.

Mumsnet, '6 ways to teach your kids about road safety', http://www.mumsnet.com/education/school-gate/features/tips-for-teaching-road-safety

Myers, SM, 'An Interactive Model of Religiosity Inheritance: The Importance of Family Context', *American Sociological Review*, 61 (5) (1996), pp. 858-866.

NatCen, 'British Social Attitudes: Church of England decline has accelerated in past decade' 2015, http://www.natcen.ac.uk/news-media/press-releases/2015/may/british-social-attitudes-church-of-england-decline-has-accelerated-in-past-decade/

Nelsen, HM, 'Religious Transmission Versus Religious Formation: Preadolescent-Parent Interaction', *The Sociological Quarterly*, 21 (1980), pp. 207-218.

Okagaki, L and Bevis, C, 'Transmission of Religious Values: Relations Between Parents' and Daughters' Beliefs', *Journal of Genetic Psychology*, 160 (3) (1999), pp. 303-318.

Oman, D, 'Spiritual Modeling and the Social Learning of Spirituality and Religion', in KI Pargament (ed.), *APA Handbook of Psychology, Religion, and Spirituality, Volume 1: Context, Theory and Research*, (Washington, DC: American Psychological Association, 2013), pp. 187-204.

Ozorak, EW, 'Social and Cognitive Influences on the Development of Religious Beliefs and Commitment in Adolescence', *Journal for the Scientific Study of Religion*, 28 (4) (1989), pp. 448- 463.

Parker, M and Gaier, E, 'Religion, Religious Beliefs, and Religious Practices among Conservative Jewish Adolescents', *Adolescence*, 15 (58) (1980), pp. 361-374.

Petts, RJ and Knoester, C, 'Parents' Religious Heterogamy and Children's Well-Being', *Journal for the Scientific Study of Religion*, 46 (3) (2007), pp. 373-389.

Ploch, DR and Hastings, DW, 'Effects of Parental Church Attendance, Current Family Status, and Religious Salience on Church Attendance', *Review of Religious Research,* 39 (4) (1998), pp. 309-320.

Potvin, RH and Sloane, DM, 'Parental Control, Age, and Religious Practice', *Review of Religious Research*, 27 (1) (1985), pp. 3-14.

Regnerus, MD, Smith, C and Smith, B, 'Social Context in the Development of Adolescent Religiosity', *Applied Developmental Science*, 8 (1) (2004), pp. 27-38.

Regnerus, MD and Uecker, JE, 'Finding Faith, Losing Faith: The Prevalence and Context of Religious Transformations during Adolescence', *Review of Religious Research*, 47 (3) (2006), pp. 217-237.

Richards, LO, *Children's Ministry: Nurturing Faith within the Family of God* (Grand Rapids: Zondervan, 1983).

Richter, P and Francis, LJ, *Gone but not Forgotten: Church Leaving and Returning* (London: Darton, Longman and Todd, 1998).

Roberts, KA and Yamane, D, *Religion in Sociological Perspective* (5th ed.) (London: SAGE, 2012).

Sandomirsky, S and Wilson, J, 'Processes of Disaffiliation: Religious Mobility among Men and Women', *Social Forces*, 68 (1990), pp. 1211-1229.

Schwartz, KD, 'Transformations in Parent and Friend Faith Support Predicting Adolescent's Religious Faith', *The International Journal for the Psychology of Religion,* 16 (4) (2006), pp. 311-32.

Scourfield, J et al., *Muslim Childhood: Religious Nurture in a European Context* (Oxford: OUP, 2013).

Scourfield, J et al., 'Religious Nurture in British Muslim Families: Implications for Social Work', *International Social Work,* 56 (3) (2013), pp. 326-342.

Sherkat, DE and Wilson, J, 'Preferences, Constraints, and Choices in Religious Markets: An Examination of Religious Switching and Apostasy', *Social Forces*, 73 (1995), pp. 993-1026.

Singh, J, 'Keeping the Faith: Reflections on Religious Nurture among young British Sikhs', *Journal of Beliefs & Values*, 33 (3) (2012), pp. 369-383.

Singleton, A, *Religion, Culture and Society: A Global Approach* (London: SAGE, 2014).

Sinha, JW, Cnaan, RA, Gelles, RJ, 'Adolescent Risk Behaviors and Religion: Findings from a National Study', *Journal of Adolescence*, 30 (2007), pp. 231-249.

Smith, C 'Is Moral Therapeutic Deism the New Religion of American Youth? Implications for the Challenge of Religious Socialization and Reproduction', in James L Heft, SM (ed.), *Passing on the Faith: Transforming Traditions for the Next Generation of Jews, Christians, and Muslims* (New York: Fordham University Press, 2006), pp. 55-74.

Smith, C and Denton, ML, Soul Searching: *The Religious and Spiritual Lives of American Teenagers* (New York: OUP, 2005).

Smith, C and Snell, P, *Souls in Transition: The Religious and Spiritual Lives of Emerging Adults*, (Oxford: OUP, 2009).

Soenke, M, Landau, MJ and Greenberg, J, 'Sacred Armor: Religion's Role as a Buffer Against the Anxieties of Life and the Fear of Death', in KI Pargament (ed.), *APA Handbook of Psychology, Religion and Spirituality: Volume 1 Context, Theory and Research* (Washington, DC: American Psychological Association, 2013), pp. 105-122.

Spencer, N et al., *Religion and Well-Being: Assessing the Evidence* (London: Theos, 2016).

Stonehouse, C, *Joining Children on the Spiritual Journey: Nurturing a Life of Faith* (Grand Rapids: Baker Books, 1998).

Strhan, A, 'Evangelical Anglicans and the Formation of Children in Modern Britain', A Day (ed.), *Contemporary Issues in the Worldwide Anglican Communion* (Farnham: Ashgate, 2016), pp. 39-53.

Taris, TW and Semin, GR, 'Passing on the Faith: How Mother-Child Communication Influences Transmission of Moral Values', *Journal of Moral Education*, 26 (2) (1997), pp. 211-221.

The Church of England, 'Generation Y has a faint cultural memory of Christianity but is not hostile towards religion, five-year study reveals', 4 October 2010, https://www.churchofengland.org/media-centre/news/2010/10/pr8610.aspx

The Church of Scotland, 'New research reveals Britain's Christian community considerably larger than expected', 24 March 2016, http://www.churchofscotland.org.uk/news_and_events/news/recent/new_research_reveals_britains_christian_community_considerably_larger_than_expected

The Woolf Institute, *Report of the Commission on Religion and Belief in Public Life. Living with Difference: Community, Diversity and the Common Good* (Cambridge: The Woolf Institute, 2015), https://corablivingwithdifference.files.wordpress.com/2015/12/living-with-difference-online.pdf

Thompson, GC, Keeping Close to Home: *The Faith and Retention of Presbyterian Emerging Adult in Northern Ireland*, Unpublished PhD Thesis (London: King's College, 2012).

Voas, D, 'Explaining Change over Time in Religious Involvement', S Collins-Mayo and P Dandelion (eds.), *Religion and Youth* (Farnham: Ashgate, 2010), pp. 25-32.

Voas, D, 'Religious Involvement over the Life Course: Problems of Measurement and Classification', *Longitudinal and Life Case Studies*, 6 (2015), pp. 212-227.

Voas, D and Watt, L *The Church Growth Research Programme Report on Strands 1 and 2: Numerical Change in Church Attendance: National, Local and Individual Factors*, 2014, http://www.churchgrowthresearch.org.uk/UserFiles/File/Reports/Report_Strands_1_2_rev2.pdf.

Voas, D and Crockett, A, 'Religion in Britain: Neither Believing nor Belonging', *Sociology*, 39 (1) (2005), pp. 11-28.

Voas, D and Storm, I, 'The Intergenerational Transmission of Churchgoing in England and Australia', *Review of Religious Research*, 53 (2012), pp. 377-395.

Wink, P et al., 'Religiousness, Spiritual Seeking, and Personality: Findings from a Longitudinal Study', *Journal of Personality*, 75 (2007), pp. 1051 – 1071.

Worsley, H, 'Conversion: A New Paradigm', *Childrenswork Magazine*, 1 (14) October 2014, pp. 22-25.

Zhai, JE et al., 'Parental Divorce and Religious Involvement among Young Adults', *Sociology of Religion*, 68 (2) (2007), pp. 125-144.